Capgemini invent

Hack the ~~design~~ system

Revolutionize the way your organization scales design

Sponsored by

Adobe

idean
Part of Capgemini Invent

This book belongs to:

_____

_____

_____

_____

Capgemini invent

Hack the ~~design~~ system

Revolutionize the way your organization scales design

Sponsored by

Edition 1.0
First published by Idean Publishing in 2019
Copyright © Idean and Capgemini Invent
Sponsored by Adobe

ISBN: 978-1-7330511-2-5

Edited by Mindy Reyes
Written by Elisa Pyrhönen
Designed by Maria Knutsson,
Benedikte Torgersen & Felipe Villarreal

Contributor-in-chief: Pierre-Henri Clouin

Full list of contributors can be found in the appendix.

All rights reserved. This book is published subject to the condition that it shall not be resold or otherwise circulated without express permission of the publisher.

idean.com/learn

Capgemini Invent helps CxOs envision and build what's next for their organizations. Located in more than 30 offices and 22 creative studios around the world, its 6,000+ strong team combines strategy, technology, data science, and creative design to develop the digital solutions and business models of the future.

Capgemini Invent is an integral part of **Capgemini** – a global leader in consulting, technology services, and digital transformation. Building on its 50-year heritage and deep industry expertise, Capgemini enables organizations to realize their business ambitions through an array of services from strategy to operations. Capgemini is driven by the conviction that the business value of technology comes from and through people. It's a multicultural company of 200,000 team members in over 40 countries. The Group reported 2018 global revenues of €13.2 billion.

Idean joined Capgemini in 2017 as its design and creative arm. They've since grown to over 700 designers across 22 cities, transforming businesses through design-led practices and helping them create more meaningful products and services.

Adobe is changing the world through digital experiences. For more information, visit www.adobe.com

Contents

Intro

Welcome	13
Why this book?	16
Who is this book for?	18
Getting started with design systems	20
Success Story - ABB	34

Part 1. The impact of a design system

The ultimate value of consistency	50
Reducing internal pain-points and inefficiencies	56
Creating a shared taste for great solutions	58
Encouraging and enabling cross-functional collaboration	66
Shifting the focus of your product teams	70
Establishing the means to showcase your successes	80
Success story - Adobe	85

Part 2. Making it a success

Design systems are made for people	100
Becoming a part of everyday operations	106
Taking portfolio management into account	112
Learning to handle incoming contributions	122

Scaling with pilots, building in feedback loops	**132**
Communication is a deal breaker	**138**
It's a custom solution that fits your organization	**150**
Maintaining design systems	**154**
Success story - Centrica	**164**

Part 3. The future of design systems

What's your next move?	**180**
Questions to chart the future of design systems	**182**
Concluding words - Our recipe	**198**

Appendix

A bit of terminology	**204**
Our Interviewees	**210**
Contributors	**219**

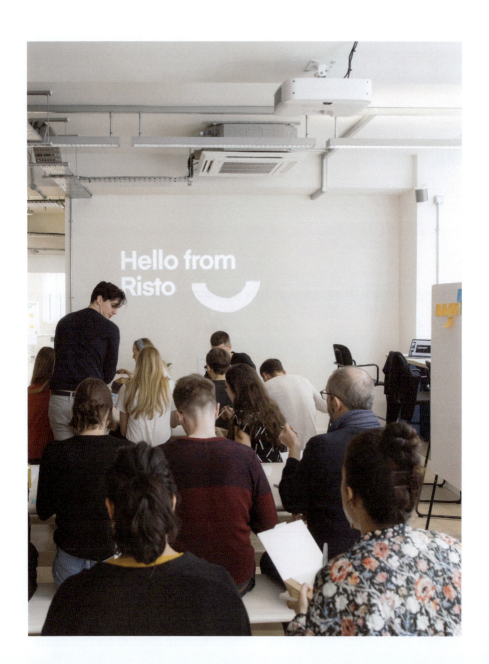

Intro

"People are the most powerful driving force for change and adoption."

Risto Lähdesmäki, CEO at Idean

Welcome

Idean is turning 20 this year. Throughout our journey, we've done thousands of design projects for a wide range of clients. In many ways, our engagements on design systems have been our most impactful work, touching thousands of products and services, tens of thousands of employees, and many many more of our clients customers and users. We've seen our clients significantly transform their product and service experiences as a result of their teams becoming so much more productive AND creative.

At Idean, our design philosophy is deeply rooted in human centricity. When we create design systems, it's second nature for us to think deeply about the many types of users a design system will serve. The brand and marketing team guiding brand expression, the product team using and leveraging the system to create product and service experiences, as well as the organization's end users and customers using these products and services.

People are the most powerful driving force for change and adoption, and they're front and center in how we approach design systems from the initial inception through their use and evolution.

"The design system provides the structure and the underlying experiential through line that unites our products."

Shawn Cheris, Director of Design, Adobe

We've partnered with Adobe on this critical and fascinating topic because we share the same vision about the power of design systems to amplify brands, accelerate transformation, and unlock creativity and productivity for teams. Through Adobe and Idean's combined networks, Idean's design systems experts were able to interview an impressive group of design leaders that are actively leading design systems.

I hope you'll enjoy reading this book and learning from it as much as I did. In particular, I hope that it serves as an inspiration to design leaders and practitioners, helping them with practical insights to advance design in their organization. I also hope that this book will inspire product executives, innovation leaders, and business owners, helping them amplify their vision and accelerate the digital transformation they're leading. And, as always, feel free to reach out with thoughts, feedback, and ideas!

Enjoy reading!
Risto Lähdesmäki, CEO at Idean

Why this book?

There are already plenty of resources available on design systems, but we haven't seen enough materials that address the human aspects, the way it shapes your organization or its outcomes. **Hack the design system** provides fresh perspectives around design systems, further contributing to the current conversations happening in the design community.

How did we get here?
To dig even deeper into the patterns that define the success of a design system, we've reached out to our friends and extended network, as well as our fellow Ideanists to gain their latest insights and thoughts on design systems.

In our interviews with these thought leaders and leading practitioners, you can read about their point of views on what role design systems play in their organizations, their journey towards the creation of their system, their approach to collaboration, and the effects they have seen - be it the impact on ways of working, or end user experience, or the bottom line.

Every design system is different and unique to every organization.
A design system needs to be the right fit because it's going to change the way things are done. It always needs to take the starting point and broader context of the organization into account.

Design systems are about people.
People that want to make an impact on the quality of their products, invest in better communication and decision-making, and the people who use the products and services.

Design systems only evolve and remain resilient because of the people involved.

How this book is organized

This book had three parts. While you most certainly can skim the book to land on any part or section, it's most beneficial to read the introduction first. Each part also includes exercises and ends with a success story to leave you with further inspiration.

Part 1: The impact of design systems
This part of the book explores the impact that a design system has on a company—the impact on internal collaboration, the end-user experience, and the effect design systems have on creativity.

Part 2: Making it into a success
A design system's success depends on its adoption: the more people that contribute to its creation and take ownership, the better. Once pilot teams are onboard, they can start leveraging customer success metrics and gather clear stated objectives.

Part 3: The future of design systems
In the future, we'd like to build the gap between digital and non-digital experiences and draw up questions around the changing digital landscape, like what does the interaction beyond the UI look like?

Who is this book for?

In bringing this together, we had two types of audiences in mind:

- Design leaders and practitioners, who want practical insights to advance design in their organizations
- Product executives, innovation leaders, and business owners, who are looking for ways to amplify and accelerate the digital transformation they're leading

Use this book for inspiration towards a more meaningful vision for your organization — one where not only your business and its customers benefit, but your employees as well.

Getting started with design systems

At Idean, when it comes to defining a design system in depth, we say that a design system is a living system of guidelines, reusable code and design assets, and tools that helps organizations deliver consistent, on-brand experiences at scale and over time.

Most typically, design systems are built, used, and maintained by product teams, who refer to it when making daily design decisions, or when implementing solutions in code. Design systems also serve multiple products over several business units.

One famous example of a design system is Google's Material Design, that's heavily used by Google, but also by external Android developers who build experiences for their platform. In this case, Material design increases cohesion across applications for the Android user, speeds up app developers work, and reinforces Google's brand value.

The main benefits of a design system are:

- Deliver strong brand identity across all touch points
- Enable change in work culture
- Save time and money
- Increase consistency
- Decrease maintenance
- Facilitate communication
- Improve user experience through well-defined and learned behaviors

A comprehensive design system should contain:

- Principles and goals
- Brand identity assets
- Functional patterns (design and code)
- Guidelines (for UX, UI, tech)
- Tools (UI kit, pattern library, and more)
- Examples and best practices

"A design system is more powerful than it appears. It's like a trojan horse going into a big organization to ignite bigger cultural change."

Jordan Fisher, Design Director at Idean

What is a design system?

"I think it's really about the long-term vision of products."

– J F Grossen, VP of Design, Global, HERE Technologies

"It's an operating system but for user experiences."

– Jeoff Wilks, Director, Carbon Design System, IBM

"It's a product that serves other products. It's an enabler for the organization. It makes the production of service creation efficient and harmonizes the products."

– Petri Heiskanen, SVP of Design, Idean

> "In a business, a design system plays the role of a facilitator and curator – it gives you that historical consciousness of what's been done in the past while allowing you to be deliberate about how you design for the future."
>
> – Hayley Hughes,
> Design Lead, Airbnb

> "It facilitates a lot of things that went wrong previously."
>
> – Kevin van der Bijl,
> Design Lead, Idean

What is it not?

"It's not a magic glue that fixes everything."

– Kevin van der Bijl,
Design Lead, Idean

"A design system is not a thing you do and then move onto the next thing. It's something that requires a lot of diligence to take care of it and to use it the way that it was intended."

– Nathan Mitchell, Design Manager and Chief Interaction Designer, National Instruments

"The design system is just a small piece of a bigger effort. It is for a company that understands the value of design. I feel a lot of people might think that the design system is the solution that is going to fix all the problems in an organization, especially in terms of consistency. But for me, a system is not about consistency. It's not about making sure that all the buttons are blue, it's about creating a cohesive experience."

– Emanuela Damiani,
Senior UX Product Designer, Mozilla

"The design system
can't be a bottleneck."

– Josh Baron,
Senior Principal Product Designer, Dell

Two complementary approaches to design systems

The user experience approach

- Getting the latest, shared, reusable assets and tools into the hands of digital teams
- Creating a core foundation for a design language across the organization
- Aligning and upskilling teams (or units) on how to make the desired user experience (UX) happen
- Sparking discussions on what else might be needed to reach a more holistic understanding of customers and other end users
- Measuring internal adoption, internal gains, and the impact on end user experiences

The transformation approach

- Ensuring a system becomes both stable enough and agile enough to roll out changes to different products and services
- Crystallizing the design system's governance model and communication strategy across the organization
- Aligning and upskilling teams (or units) on the desired changes, including adjusted behavior and roles
- Sparking discussions on what else might be needed to reach the stated vision
- Measuring the impact of the system in light of more extensive, transformation initiatives

27

Who should be involved in a design system initiative?

Product/service organizations

The people that create and manage products and services need to work together so the system can make it out into the "real world." When these teams collaborate, it will clearly show in the customer-facing solutions. A product/service organization usually has a mix of internal and external staff, as well as a wide range of experts from various fields. If the organization has more complex platforms, e.g., white-label products and several B2B solutions, a wider range of people extend out even further.

Senior-level staff and end users

What goes into the system should be validated by either those who lead the design system initiative or the final decision makers. Also, there are many involved the end user research, brand research, customer insights, analytics, sales, marketing, testing, and customer services, and these people might not use the design system every day. Having a constant feedback loop of actionable customer insights flowing into the system can significantly raise its value.

Brand

It's not just about the core brand assets. If we don't have a holistic understanding of the desired brand perception and audiences, it's hard to translate internal definitions across all the different touchpoints accurately. For brand units that are more associated with marketing than the products and services themselves, it's a perfect opportunity to start bridging that gap.

Other business stakeholders

Legal, backend services, HR, and internal communications all have a stake in a design system even if it's not on a day-to-day basis. The same thing applies when involving any of the other previously mentioned units. Having a benchmark awareness of the shared goals and suitable ways to get involved can help to shift the focus forward, beyond the way things have run before.

> **Tip**
>
> If you find yourself repeating, "it's not just for designers," maybe it's time to call it a service/product system, or an experience system instead.
>
> - Most organizations give their system a name that ties it to their brand or organization
> - For example, Adobe's Spectrum, ABB's CommonUX, and Centrica's Nucleus

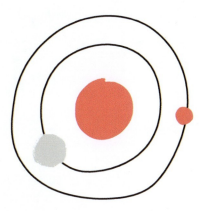

Five stages in the life of a design system

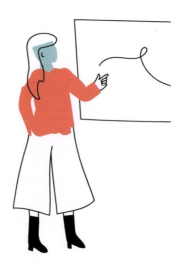

For the system curators:

1. Researching and getting initial buy-in
2. Making it through the first months; building solid starting points while testing them early and often
3. Ensuring early-stage adoption and growth
4. Broadening the scope and making it more stable
5. Balancing major releases and smaller updates to the shared assets and rituals

For the makers leveraging the system:

1. First potential advocates and partner units engaged in the philosophy and objectives
2. Primary users learning more about the principles and getting the first glimpses of what it might mean in practice
3. Early successes raise interest, as well as questions, suggestions, and worries; more people and units become involved
4. Changes start to appear in more products and services, leveraging the system to varying degrees
5. New initiatives and changes begin to roll in as time and energy are freed up

Jeoff Wilks
Director of Carbon
Design System, IBM

Jeoff Wilks, IBM on how to get started building a design system

"To me, the easiest way to get buy-in and budget for a design system is to create one. And so that begs the question, "Well, how do we get the budget to create a design system?" Well, first of all, you need to have enough designers and front-end developers to create it. For teams that don't have that, they could look at a system like Carbon as an upstream, and then customize it to their needs.

One way or another, you need to create an initial asset and convince the organization, "Look, we have this design system that only one or two people have initially created, but the teams that are using it are seeing results. They see an acceleration in their development cycle, and they see a lot better quality in the user experience." Those are the two metrics that you need to move the needle on.

Maybe you have ten designers. Is that enough to have a design system? I would argue that having ten designers might mean you have fewer products, and so the answer is yes. If you have ten designers, you could have two people working half the time on a design system. Or if you're an even smaller company with four designers, you could have one or two people working a quarter of the time on a design system.

In my opinion, there's always room to create a design system no matter what your current design budget is. Now, how do you take it a step further to where your business knows that there is a dedicated design system team, and people are okay with it?

If the initial design team has been trying to make some of their work systematic in the form of a smaller design system, and it's causing acceleration and quality improvement in products, then at some point, the business is going to say, "we want more of that." And so then it becomes effortless to have a budget conversation. Sometimes the business tells you, "hey, your budget's going to go up. We need more of that design system stuff. So, you're getting a couple of extra people, figure out what to do with them.""

Intro

ABB

Industry
Manufacturing and Engineering

Employees
147k

Headquarters
Zurich, Switzerland

Design system creation
14 months

Humanizing technology

How an industrial heavyweight created a UX foundation for its digital products

ABB is a global technology leader that has started the journey to humanize its technology with a systematic design approach to develop coherent, powerful and enabling solutions that provide meaningful experiences to their customers.

"We have a strong need to offer our technology in a more humanized way to enable our customers and users to take full advantage of our digital offering. UX design is the key element to meet this need."

Marjukka Mäkelä, Head of UX Design, Digital ABB

As digitalization is influencing even the most complex areas of the industrial domains in an ever-increasing pace, established technology pioneers like ABB are looking for new ways to take their digital offering to the next level when it comes to the ease of use and consistency in brand experience.

In 2017, a small group of managers realized that a great user-experience (UX) design can play a pivotal role in sustaining a brand's position in competitive digitally-driven markets. At that time, work on a new ABB Ability Platform™ was only starting and customer facing interfaces were at a nascent stage. Previous efforts in UX had proven valuable, and it was high time to join distributed design forces and find a common voice, a common system, that guided everyone in the digital design.

Together with Idean, ABB started the CommonUX Design System initiative: establishing a dedicated team with a versatile design system, providing ABB product teams and partners a set of shared principles, tools and methodologies to steer everyone towards a collective ABB voice that connects both design and content to the brand.

Kickstarting the journey

A journey of a thousand miles begins with a single step. For ABB, this meant trowelling deep into the expansive landscape of ABB portfolio of a thousand products and understanding diverse product team needs in the 147,000 employee organization.

A better understanding of ABB's culture helped the team to create an ambitious plan. The inspiration came from the collaboration with different stakeholders, and efforts were made to deliver a story of the emerging system. A baseline set of UI components was drafted to set everyone on the same page with bold style characteristics.

Sucess Story - ABB

Starting from the deep end

One of the main goals was to define and carefully select the products that could spearhead the initiative. By demonstrating their potential to a broader audience within the organization, it would make them possible to replicate and adopt in other projects.

At ABB, this meant starting at the deep end with complex products being used in highly regulated sectors. This was to help in understanding how industry standards and legislation could affect the upcoming design system.

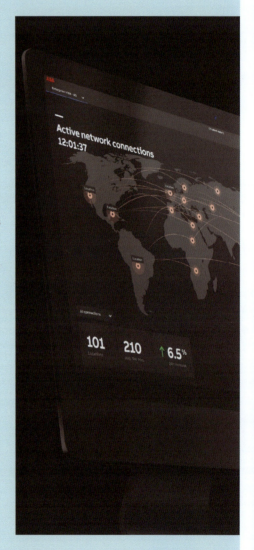

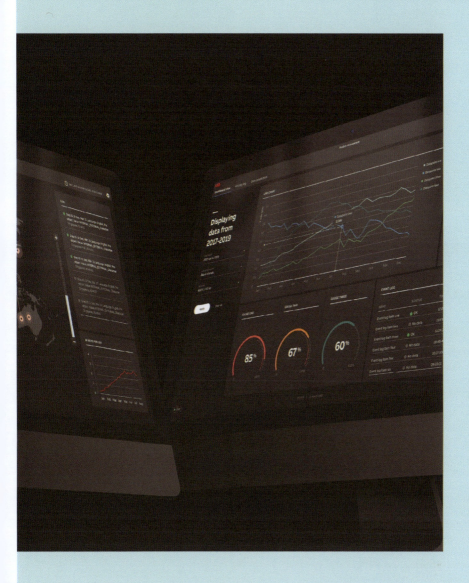

Making change exciting

The team put their efforts into making the system transparent. Collaborating with product teams and creating visceral examples of how CommonUX Design System could impact user experience in even the most complex interfaces was essential in gaining buy-in and adoption among different business units.

The team's core idea was to first create the foundation of the design system (i.e., a vision along with design principles and baseline UI component libraries), and then to start communicating it to the hundreds of ABB product teams. The promotional videos on the new site were among the first actions taken with the release of the design system in September 2018. The team wanted to create excitement through videos to showcase a better future and illustrate the abilities embedded in the human-centered design.

To be successful, the team itself needed to stand behind and believe in the system. They needed to inspire others to follow ideas of clarity, empowerment of end users and customers and the creation of brand coherence. The best examples were brought together in the form of a book, directing and strengthening the characteristics of ABB's design language.

Globally experimental

Many low-fidelity tests were conducted to understand how designs were perceived in different cultures and context. For example, the meaning of UI icons was tested with a survey, asking employees around the globe to describe what metaphors they associated with the icons. This information allowed us to create an aligned icon library with shared metaphors, sizes, and guidelines suitable for all UI's designed within ABB.

Success Story - ABB

Enabling collaboration

The small but dynamic community of designers at ABB was involved in the creation of the design system from the very beginning. The design community focused early on engagement models to allow everyone to contribute to the system more productively and help accelerate and scale the system adoption faster. The complex industrial solutions require domain knowledge that is efficiently accessible within the business units.

CommonUX Design System was aimed to empower designers and developers to execute the human-centered design in their everyday work. The central UX design team needed to closely collaborate with tens of business units and apply a positive service mindset to its practices.

A snapshot of survey results

69%

Of respondents believed that the harmonization of user interfaces and consistency within software products would have a positive impact on sales.

63%

Of respondents mentioned that they needed to follow some industry-specific regulations when creating interfaces.

80%

Of respondents felt that applying CommonUX would ensure that the products are on brand.

Running a survey each quarter supports the evaluation of the current state and impact of the system. It also helps with mapping awareness levels and unmet needs.

(Participants: 107 participants from every division, from at least 14 countries, 86% ABB and 14% externals)

What's next?

- CommonUX is still young and evolving, and more content creation is still on the way.
- Starting from the tangible assets and constant engagement within the organization has paved the way for creation of a design system.
- Keeping up the momentum and increasing internal awareness of the system.
- With more contributors and participants joining in, it's natural to focus on evolving the ways of working.
- Training materials will help increase adoption at scale.

Part 1

The impact of a design system

A design system increases efficiency and creates a bigger cultural impact

The ultimate value of consistency

Ensuring and achieving consistency in user experience across products and platforms is the most commonly mentioned driver to start creating a design system. Inconsistency in user experience can make a business look and feel like a completely different company across different channels.

As the design system matures, consistency starts to cover more than just the user experience. Consistency can be seen in how the brand is understood within the organization, what methodologies and processes are used in product development across teams, down to the level of how components are built into the code. The design system helps the whole organization be more aligned and have one shared vision.

Increased usability and accessibility
When teams are moving fast, it's the final finishes — and in some cases the basic requirements to meet demands — that tend to suffer. With reusable components at hand, teams don't have to start from scratch each time. This means that a share of usability and accessibility issues have been solved. With further training, the team will become more aware of the choices behind the UI patterns.

Solutions, instead of individual products and services

There's a special benefit when establishing consistency for companies that serve the same customers and end users with multiple products and services. A design system helps product teams focus not just on their use cases but their customers' whole relationship with the parent brand. Even when specific products have a mind of their own, there are recurring interactions and steps that customers expect to stay the same. For customers and end users, this kind of uniformity can range from the products and services merely being more intuitive to use, all the way to opting for a suite of products because their onboarding costs are lower.

Stronger, more premium brand

A brand that is consistent with its standards of quality in its products and services is more trustworthy and valuable. Apple is a prime example of this with its strong focus on craft.

A design system is a core mechanism to scale quality standards across teams that sometimes have wildly different maturity levels. Design systems help raise the bar for what good design looks like in an organization.

A design system can express the organization's core values and influence the opinions of customers. When you put more care into the details, it shows.

How do design systems ultimately help us reach better quality?

- We have more time to craft individual components, but also spend more time finessing products and services
- We have a systemic way to continuously iterate on our components as we learn from their actual usage in different contexts
- We can ensure accessibility and legibility on a system level through color and type tokens
- We can systematize delightful micro-interactions through patterns, rules, and components, and we have more time to build and test them

> **Tip**
>
> Highlighting inconsistencies in user experience is an efficient way to showcase the need for a design system.
>
> - Prepare a shared inventory deck
> - Add slides for various types of UI elements
> - Include a few bullet points of guidance: e.g., images of current, live products
> - Invite everyone to contribute to the inventory
> - Store a copy of the deck
> - Rerun the exercise again after a few months to see any changes

Increasing consistency to speed up implementation

> *"We sell business solutions, which typically means customers are buying several products that all need to be working together."*
>
> – J F Grossen, VP of Design, Global, HERE Technologies

> *"Two years ago, our CEO said that it felt like we changed banks when we changed channels. When using the website, the app, or the portal, it didn't feel like the same bank across all channels."*
>
> – Marie Petit, Leader of the UX Chapter, Crédit Agricole Technologies & Services

"We're working hard to ensure that everyday work accrues to the company's priorities so that everything we're doing can have the broadest impact."

– Joseph McLaughlin, Partner, Director of Design, Microsoft

"If you were a user of more than one of these well-designed—but not cohesive—experiences, you would have to learn new navigation paradigms and new interaction models for doing similar things across applications."

– Nick Cochran, Design Practices Lead, ExxonMobil

Hayley Hughes on accessibility

Hayley Hughes,
Design Lead, Airbnb

"Design systems, broadly speaking, are decisions that are manifested and governed to scale across an organization. This means that in the future, they can account for even bigger decisions made about different steps and touch points along a user's journey. Service design is not deeply considered in design systems today. When you go a level higher, the decisions around a company's ethos and values means systems require the involvement of ethics and brand experts. Eventually, a mature design system could, in theory, influence the way a company decides or evolves its business model.

We're currently in the process of not only adding more components, but we're also evolving the visual design language and the interaction patterns of the design system. We're doubling down on our accessibility focus. It's a high priority for the company coming straight from the CEO, which is exciting.

There's an inextricable link between design systems and accessibility – and designing with people who have disabilities as part of your process. A system is a mechanism for years of scaling repeatable success. If you define success by every person's ability to access your product in the ways that work best for them, then that's what you'll scale. If you define success by how good something looks, that's what you'll scale but not much else. Defining success upfront determines the impact you make with systems. On top of all that, success is also dependent on teams using the components in the first place. So, you must also define success by something so inspirational that teams will want to use the system. I would focus on fundamental human rights like access as a starting place.

It's important for us to encourage teams to use system components and create variations of them as opposed to coding already existing components from scratch. Design tokens and themes enable variety without sacrificing consistency. We support teams building brand new components from scratch, and those are brought back into the system through a contribution model. Helping teams understand the difference between a variation and a brand new component is critical because accessibility and performance regressions increase when teams believe coding everything from scratch is faster than making variations in the system.

A system has a moral imperative, whether you design for it or not. When designing a product with good intent, it's important to define what "good" is, imagine the opposite (bad intent), as well as every scenario in between where it might be repurposed, hacked, or misused. At Airbnb, our employees also use our platform. They are also hosts and guests, so they have to challenge biases intentionally, so they aren't just designing for themselves.

We're investing in inclusive design. People with disabilities who work at Airbnb and live in our local community design with us and test our product. We also have a team focused on anti-discrimination and the designers who work on that team help us reduce the discrimination in our product and in the experience of being an employee as much as possible."

Reducing internal pain points and inefficiencies

A design system is designed to stay. Growing from a small investment to something that can feel big and expensive wouldn't be possible without exponentially higher returns in the long-term.

Reducing your time (and cost) to market

Standardizing shared styles and components influences the product organization first, and then ripples throughout the company.

Having a shared UI foundation means that assets can work effortlessly together from the get-go. It makes it possible for teams to spend more time creating and validating alternative flows. You can see these benefits in the early stages of the process.

Furthermore, less time is spent documenting and meeting over detailed specifications. After all, the sources for the latest assets and styles are already there. Having fewer custom implementations means reducing both the complexity of code and the number of bugs, which then leads to avoiding less unpleasant surprises down the line.

Build happier, more productive teams
A well-implemented design system is easy to understand and use if and when it:

- Supports individuals and teams in their daily work
- Provides an absolute benchmark for quality, as well as a clear rationale behind the decisions made
- Provides both velocity and stability

As a result, onboarding new team members is easier, bringing efficiencies to a new team member's first day. Designers and developers, as well as all their closest stakeholders, have an easier time discussing potential changes. A number of alignment questions that previously went unanswered are now answered right away. Checking recommendations are made easy. Beyond having shared guidance, teams can increase their focus on core objectives. Seeing more progress is not only rewarding for the team; it makes it more likely for decisions to be bolder and more ambitious.

"A design system allows everyone to work in parallel: copywriters, designers, developers, project managers. You don't waste any more time in meetings on small details. Designers can focus on connecting with people and developers on performance, better quality and more advanced solutions."

– Robin Klein Schiphorst,
Design Lead, Idean

Creating a shared taste for great solutions

An organization's mission, vision, strategy, and brand are embedded throughout the organization. They are widely accepted and are at the core of everything the organization stands for.

Or are they?

The bigger the organization is, the more specialized experts there tend to be, the more activities there are, and the harder it becomes to define what the great solutions are. As a result, solutions and decisions are pulled into several directions with each iteration, review, and sign-off along the way.

Bridging concepts and practice
A design system provides shared decision-making criteria. Some of these are high-level, such as conceptual philosophy and principles. Some are embedded in the technical and design choices of reusable assets, and some are embedded in the insights and arguments behind particular decisions.

A key difference in traditional, high-level statements of key priorities is that it goes all the way to tangible, practical solutions.

Actively inviting debates of "what's good"

A design system also provides a platform to debate what's good and what's not. This is what allows everyone to propose future ideas and challenge day-to-day decisions. It's these debates and their curation - the governance of it all - that define the core of the design system in the long run.

Such discussions already take place in everyday work. A key difference here is sharing accountability: it's about having good mechanisms in place for making sure it works not just as a one-off, but proves its worth in multiple instances and for multiple teams. It's also about shifting the focus on outcomes (for the business, for end users and customers) as much as the outputs aka solutions being discussed.

Governance
A design system provides teams with everything that is needed to create great solutions that will benefit the customer. Providing the right amount of governance and shared ownership will empower teams to work with the design system.

> **Tip**
>
> Channeling all disciplines:
> - Keep identifying the shared evaluation criteria embedded in your design system
> - Find ways to keep these present in the right moments in everyday decision-making

But what is the right amount of governance? Will shared ownership work when ten teams are working on different parts of the solution?

Every design system needs a form of governance embedded in the processes and tools. This ensures the survival of the design system over time and builds a culture of collaboration; teams will need to spend more time communicating with internal stakeholders and potential partners.

Reducing the knowledge gap
A design system can become a shared knowledge base for the entire organization. It brings best practices and most up-to-date learnings into a single source, and helps reduce the knowledge gaps between teams.

A design system is also a catalyst for change: as much of the tactical UI asset work is reduced, your teams may need to take on new tasks-like research-that require new capabilities. So while a design system brings harmony and increases maturity across teams, it may also reveal capability gaps that you didn't know existed.

Tip

Make tools, not rules.
- Philosophy and principles define a shared direction, not the solution
- Shared components and styles are best served with a clear purpose and some built-in flexibility
- Documentation makes it possible to provide insights that are hard to derive from the assets alone, but it's soon discarded if it doesn't serve the needs of busy practitioners
- Discussions and hands-on practice are often more effective for onboarding than any documentation on its own

Positioning the design system within the organization

"A design system is the enabler to change the work culture and start the right conversations. It allows everyone in the organization to understand the purpose of their role and how they can participate in creating great solutions."

– Kevin van der Bijl,
Design Lead, Idean

"A design system can be the one constant thing in that conversation that everyone can come back to and use as a source of truth."

– Nathan Mitchell, Design Manager and
Chief Interaction Designer,
National Instruments

Iterating ideas based on shared principles

Principles become product reality only if a wide range of people know and understand them well. With practice and iteration, people can feel that there are many ways in which these principles can be applied.

Goal

To keep the shared principles top-of-mind in everyday decision-making.

Steps

1. Take a look at your high-level principles.
2. Prepare a large, one-page paper for each set of your principles.
3. Make the context and purpose clear. For example, you can write "The Experience" at the top of the page and go from there.
4. Go through the more detailed definitions and keywords. Turn these into "How might we..." questions. For example, How might we tailor these to people?
5. Keep the questions short and clear. If needed, add a few supporting keywords as reminders of particular things to pay attention to.
6. Make these templates available together with a "quick guide" on when and how to best use them.

Tip

- Using questions instead of rule-like definitions makes a session feel more empowering. As a result, there's a chance of seeing more creative outcomes.

- Add enough space between the questions. Even if you're not running it as a post-it exercise, the space is a physical representation of "making space" for alternative ideas.

- If you have multiple sets of principles, aka multiple pages, pick only one, or a few, for a single session to give each question the proper time and focus.

- It's not necessary to refer to the principles all the time (there will always be a long list of other criteria to consider), but regular check-ins are recommended.

Follow up with one of these activities

- Use this workshop template in reviews and critiques.
- Use this workshop template in ideation.
- It's good to share the most effective designs and solutions that have gone live, as these can be presented in the design system as specific examples.
- If a principle definition is repeatedly proven as irrelevant or ineffective, it's necessary to check if this is a case-specific exception or a broader, shared issue.

Encouraging and enabling cross-functional collaboration

Design systems create a common language across the organization. Part of it relies on a conscious effort to cut across silos. The other part is a natural result of the activities required for setting up a design system.

Including multiple perspectives
Creating and running a design system requires buy-in across the organization. A design system is going to set some shared rules and values, even new ways of working. Sometimes it's possible to build on existing ones and sometimes it's essential to encourage new ones. A design system provides a platform for this essential redesign.

A design system should also be intuitive, allowing anyone to pick it up and use it in their daily work. Getting to this point requires spending time with different units and disciplines.

A shared point of reference
A user should feel that a brand is recognizable across all touchpoints, whether it's a marketing campaign or a checkout flow. Visual guidelines or core brand assets are not enough. It requires involving multiple functions.

An official, centralized resource makes it easier for other units and teams to flag recurring issues they're passionate about and regularly dealing with. At the same time, a design system will bring to light new shared knowledge that used to sit within other disciplines and units.

Creating the time to collaborate internally

A broader consensus of the shared principles and priorities tends to make the discussions during sign-offs and gate reviews better. Having ready-made, on-brand assets helps product teams and managers create mockups faster. This also means it's easier to facilitate early stage ideation, collaboration, and user validation.

Having modern tools and processes helps people to work more in parallel, further helping different disciplines and units to collaborate better. When work is done more efficiently, teams have more time to work together and learn from each other, and the design system helps them speak the same language.

> **Tip**
>
> Training sessions, demos, reviews, etc. are a perfect excuse to start inviting members from other disciplines.
>
> - Don't try to cover everything in one meeting, but focus on your topics. For example, have social meetups around the official, latest guidelines
> - Share invites to open-door sessions where you answer questions
> - At the end of the session, chat with new participants: e.g., Was it useful for them? What knowledge do they have that would benefit the system?

Investing in a design system means investing in communication

"In a large organization, it's hard to have communication and collaboration across all digital products. So, design systems can help with that."

– Josh Baron,
Senior Principal Product Designer, Dell

"The biggest impact is that we all speak the same design language in a meeting even if we come from different parts of the organization."

– Emanuela Damiani,
Senior UX Product Designer, Mozilla

"One of the benefits I didn't anticipate was that people really came together."

– Nick Cochran, Design Practices Lead, ExxonMobil

"I see better or stronger collaboration between designers and developers. They have the same vision that's very aligned whenever they have to talk about or explain the interface to a product owner."

– Marie Petit, Leader of the UX Chapter, Crédit Agricole Technologies & Services

Part 1 **70**

Shift the focus of your product teams towards value

Congratulations! Your product teams are now working more efficiently as a result of having a shared foundation and shared assets to build on.

So now, how are you going to invest that saved time and energy? What are the new things to consider to manage your teams successfully?

We've identified several different answers to these questions.

Scale up a design organization
An organization determined to raise the number of its digital teams will be in a much better position to do so.

Document everything
Whether it's embedded in the tools, lives on a public site, and made widely available, documentation helps with the onboarding process.

Shape the culture with community-building activities
In a big community, the areas that are not covered by the design system need to be developed as soon as possible, such as hiring and career paths. If DevOps and DesignOps teams are already in place (or any other suitable operations management model), great. If not, it's time to start investigating.

Invest in more senior experts
We might also see a shift towards smaller teams. Reducing the overall headcount is a clear monetary benefit.

This also makes it possible to focus on hiring more senior experts or those who thrive in a collaborative, cross-disciplinary culture.

Lead with outcomes
Teams are more naturally able to do what they were meant to do all along: produce excellent results through considered, well-positioned outputs.

For management (and the teams), the question to consider is if teams' key performance indicators (KPIs) currently in place are still the right ones.

Are design systems killing creativity?

The answer depends on who you are asking.

As the governance of shared UI assets becomes centralized (and in some ways, much more distributed), there's less detailed UI work to go around within product teams. For craft driven UI experts (and the occasional product owner) this can be felt like a loss, especially if there are limited opportunities to contribute to the system.

For many UX experts (be their specialty in design or development, or otherwise), being able to produce prototypes faster and spend more time testing alternatives is an advantage. Release cycles may stay the same, but the quality and scale of changes might rise drastically.

Soon, teams will come up with solutions to deliver beyond the organization's current capabilities. This means more time is spent selling ideas internally. The better an organization can scale these bottom-up initiatives, the bigger leaps the whole organization might ultimately take.

> **Tip**
>
> A design system that's tied to live products can bring the most operational benefits. It also requires more stability and less breaking changes. To cater to that and keep a healthy flow of new perspectives:
>
> - Organize hackathons that allow individuals and teams to go wild, stepping beyond the system for a moment
> - Make sure to map not just the alternative directions, but the underlying reasons that make these enticing to the teams

> **Tip**
>
> Few design systems will cover 100% of live UI assets. Ownership of the journeys, as well as the more unique, advanced, and specialized assets, remain within the product teams.
>
> - Make it easier (and more rewarding) for teams to use existing, shared, basic assets other than creating custom versions
> - Make it easier for teams to build on the current principles and foundations, even when an asset is not (yet) part of the system

Investing saved time and energy into...

"Focus on the bigger picture, on the customer problem you're looking to solve."

– Matthew Gottschalk,
Design Operations Manager, Centrica

"Put that saved time into considering better products."

– Christian Aminoff,
Creative Director, Idean

"We're building a design system so that designers can focus on creativity, inspiration, the global layout of the screen, and the steps of the journey."

– Marie Petit, Leader of the
UX Chapter, Crédit Agricole
Technologies & Services

"Right now we're focused heavily on figuring out how to use design thinking, creativity, and collaboration as a more strategic tool for the business."

– Jason Cyr, Director,
Design Transformation, Cisco

"Enable these teams to focus on their product, category, and brand expression, but evolve the foundation together."

– Joseph McLaughlin, Director of Design, Microsoft

From...to... statements

There are always other initiatives and targets around. Aligning the design system with current causes helps drive both.

Goal

Map desired changes, painting a picture of "before" and "after."

Steps

1. Interview key stakeholders and intended users on their daily work, current bottlenecks/pain points, current initiatives/motivations, as well as expectations for the design system.
2. Summarize essential findings into "from... to" statements that help to identify what is going to change.
3. Use the summary as a part of your communication and training package.

Tip

- Focus on activities and behaviors that take place in everyday work.
- Use short but descriptive sentences, one sentence per box.
- Keep it as a single-page summary. Any more than 6-7 items becomes too much to remember. Prioritize if need be.
- You can also use the template in workshops, co-creating the statements. In this case, facilitate the session in a way that minimizes "power biases," allowing each voice to be heard.

From...	...to

Follow up with one of these activities:

- Use the summary to discuss how the design system might be used to realize the desired changes.
- Refer to the desired, future state when discussing priorities and defining metrics.
- When working with individuals and teams, keep looking out for, as well as nudging towards the desired changes.

Cheat sheet - Questions to map the current baseline

Enabling collaboration

- What's the customer experience like? (as customers describe it)?
- What's the brand perception like?
- What's the customer satisfaction rating?
- What's the usability rating?
- What's the accessibility rating?
- What's the technical performance rating?
- How much variation is there across the different products and services / different journeys?
- How much time are teams "blindly" spending on learning and running experiments vs. churning out updates?
- How many category-defining products and services are in the organization's portfolio?

Increasing productivity and efficiency

- How quickly can new, potential offerings be brought to market?
- How quickly can new features be shipped?
- How many alternative solutions/ iterations can be explored within a sprint?
- How long does it take to introduce a new view, flow, or journey for testing?
- How long does preparing and running a handover to implementation take?
- How many bugs are there?
- How much effort is required to implement changes?
- How often are basic assets re-created across the different instances, teams, and over time?
- What's the overall long haul?

Greater cross-disciplinary, cross-functional collaboration

- Is there a common language to describe what's good and what's not?
- Are there shared principles that resonate across different teams and units?
- Are these shared evaluation criteria present in reviews and sign-offs?
- Are there shared practices and rituals for makers of different kinds and specialties?
- How satisfied are designers and developers with each others' work?
- Are there ways to evolve and govern what's considered the latest and best?
- How active is the grass-root iteration and promotion within the key, strategic areas?

Nurturing talent and creativity

- How long does it take to onboard new team members?
- How big are the talent gaps between different teams?
- What is the typical "maker" profile like?
- What are the typical career tracks for "makers" like?
- What is the employee profile like?
- What do "the makers" spend most of their time on?

Establish the means to showcase your successes

Based on our interviews, it tends to take a relatively long time until there's a formal, established way of measuring a design system. Metrics evolve. Early on, anecdotal proof points might be enough, e.g., pilot teams measuring productivity and velocity with their release or leveraging existing metrics like customer success metrics. We believe that having conscious, clearly stated objectives not only helps the team make better decisions along the way; it's powerful when showcasing your successes.

"We know metrics are important, but"...
Measuring the absolute impact of a design system seems difficult. We've identified a number of reasons why this might be so:

- Prioritization: There are several, potential benefits and aspects to pick from (especially if you're an advocate).
- Built-in delays: The design system needs some solid groundwork as well as a series of roll-outs for the benefits to be felt and seen more widely.
- Scale: Most design system projects are ambitious. There's a tendency to think "wait, we haven't reached this and that milestone yet..."
- Origins: As the name suggests, design systems grew from a broad discipline. While this might be changing, designers haven't traditionally been trained on metrics and impact assessment at a higher organizational (or even a financial) level.
- No benchmark: There are no ready-set sources for it. If there is no established benchmark to compare measures against, it's harder to get to the data in the first place. It's harder to say whether to what a degree a result is good or concerning. It also requires some consideration to come up with potential samples and comparison points.
- Multiple stakeholders: Everyone values different things at different levels. When it comes to more specific goals, in particular, it's good to keep actively listening to what contributors and stakeholders value the most.

Showing up regularly

Most of the time, there is no direct pressure to show value. As long as the benefits are clear to the teams that are directly working with the system and higher management is convinced it's worth investing in, it's "good to go" ... for now.

It is good to keep explicitly stating the expected gains: What are the goals we want to achieve?

Whatever your goals, or preferred means for measuring progress, it's the regularity of your reporting that makes the difference. It can be hard in the beginning, but the only way to get better is to work at it.

> **Tip**
>
> You don't need to have super specific ways to be able to keep tabs on progress
>
> - Check-in on your goals each month
> - List what progress you've seen, heard, felt, and counted

Tip

Translate your objectives into hypotheses early on. For example:

- "Our design system will free up more time for innovation and creativity"
- "Our design system will accelerate product development"

Tip

A survey is a common way to get feedback and measure the health of the design system.

- Run a survey each quarter/regularly.
- Keep tabs on your long-term objectives as well as short-term plans.
- Don't run on numbers alone; leave in opportunities for open feedback.
- Share the good news as well as the bad. It means you're paying attention and learning.

> "The stronger the metrics are connected to the actual needs that you're trying to meet, the safer you are... Before and after comparisons can be pretty effective. If possible, calculate the cost of the current ways of working."
>
> – Christian Aminoff, Idean

Adobe

How Adobe is executing design systems at scale in a highly complex landscape

Sponsored by

Adobe

Part 1

How Adobe is executing design systems at scale in a highly complex landscape

Adobe

Industry
Digital creative media and marketing software

Employees
21,000+

Headquarters
San Jose, California

Design system implementation:
Spectrum

Adobe is a company known for its creativity software products. It has a long history in the creative industry and one that has grown its product portfolio through developing original creative tooling and through numerous acquisitions.

Shawn Cheris, who leads the Brand & Experience team within Adobe Design, shared Spectrum's story with us. In the early days, the need for a system had been apparent to the Design team for a long time. Shawn was the first one to champion the idea of a design system and get buy-in throughout the company.

Unlike many companies that have a broad product offering, Adobe products make up one big ecosystem, and so Adobe customers are often users of products across different ecosystems:

"Adobe's broad offering should have experiential consistency, and you need that confidence from us when you buy our products. Quite often, our customers use multiple Adobe products. The design system has provided a lens that reminds everyone that while their product is important, the overall experience for Adobe users is everyone's responsibility."

The early days

A vision video played a critical role in creating buy-in for the design system. This video showed a customer journey spanning all of Adobe's different ecosystems, indicating what a consistent experience would look and feel like. We asked Shawn about the journey of getting buy-in for Spectrum:

"I gave a presentation around what it was and why it was important probably a hundred times. I went to every product and engineering manager that would give me their time, and I presented it to them and helped them understand the importance and benefits of what we wanted to accomplish.

The role of the design system is to provide the structure and the underlying experiential through-line that unites our products. We do that by providing resources to help make both the designer's and the engineer's job easier. We also provide a contribution model that everybody can be a part of."

When the Photoshop team got on board with the system, that was the tipping point. With almost three decades in the market, it's a prime example of managing flagship products and staying relevant. As Shawn put it, it was both a challenge and a technical feat.

In terms of adoption, the initial focus was on two things: getting the new look and feel into all new products that were built from scratch and partnering with teams creating centralized product frameworks.

2013

Today

Nurturing Spectrum today

In the last year, Spectrum has reached a point of maturity. Adoption and familiarity are growing more and more.

"It's to the degree where you'll talk to product managers, and they'll say, "We're doing Spectrum" or "We've got Spectrum" or "We're Spectrum-ing." They won't always 100% know what Spectrum is, but they know that they're supposed to use it."

Shawn uses a gardening metaphor to explain how the design team no longer needs to make a case to Adobe product teams about using a design system:

"We're moving towards a new strategy where we're operating more like gardeners. Going forward, a lot of our efforts have grown around providing an operational model that allows us to take in all the best thinking, all the best ideas from across the company. And as people are developing new products and new product experiences, we fold their learnings back into the language in a way that is responsible and that everyone else can consume. A lot of what we do comes down to managing all the input and contributions."

As anybody who has ever nurtured a garden knows, most of it comes down to establishing the right conditions:

"The right design language gives us a consistent view of how we should present our experiences to our customers. But it can't cover every conceivable corner. And so you have to provide an opportunity for people to innovate and to add new patterns. You also need to balance that and make sure that everybody's reusing the best of what already exists and not inventing new and unnecessary stuff."

The role of designers is evolving, so are the tools

We also spoke with Cisco Guzman, who is helping to guide the direction of Adobe XD, about how design systems are shaping the tools of the trade.

"Design is about solving tough problems while creating meaningful experiences – and our methodology is remarkably simple: put the people you're designing for in the middle, create a shared understanding of those problems, iterate quickly to imagine solutions, and move as quickly as you can into implementation. XD is the collaboration platform to design and prototype engaging user experiences – whether you're one designer or an enterprise. XD helps designers and their entire organizations to build experiences together that matter."

Design systems have become a hot topic in the design and development communities for a good reason. The pressures of content velocity, continuous collaboration, and emerging platforms mean that designers and developers are working harder than ever to keep up, stay connected, and forge new frontiers. So the designers are asking themselves, "is there a better way of doing things?" A design system promises that it will help you to scale what you're doing – to create consistency and efficiency as much as you possibly can. This, in turn, means that designers can focus more time on building better experiences for their customers – and that's ultimately what builds a business.

What makes work engaging for creatives?

Creative people love solving problems. Adobe's approach, methodology, and tools all point to one thing: creating elegant solutions to tough problems while elevating the human experience. Design systems provide everyone within a team or enterprise with the building blocks to create experiences consistently and efficiently. That means that designers and developers can spend less time on the mechanics of consistency and more time digging into understanding and addressing customer problems.

From Guzman's point of view, the best design systems are flexible and straightforward. They bring people together, provide the building blocks, and then encourage designers to solve problems contextually using those building blocks. It's a language, not a canon. So the more that innovation itself is a foundational principle, the more likely that the system is adopted and grows.

"No designer is an island, and the creative process is not simply about our journey of understanding the customer. It's really about how we bring an entire organization along with us. We move fluidly between different modalities – designing, prototyping – and collaborating, at every step. That's why collaboration is built into the core of XD rather than as an afterthought."

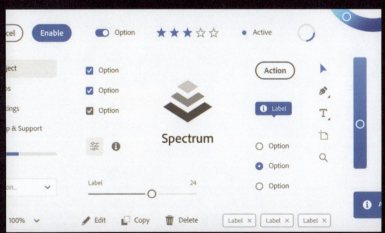

How do I create a design system?

Adobe's customers who have created design systems seem to agree on a few principles: keep it simple, and build it to evolve. When asked about how XD brings simplicity into a naturally complex area:

"One of the things we've heard from customers who have experience building design systems is that keeping it simple is essential. So simplicity is at the heart of building a design system in XD. You can start defining the colors, character styles, and components that make up your visual vocabulary in a cloud document using the assets panel.

Once that's done, you can share the source of truth with other designers – enabling them to link their cloud documents to yours. As you make changes to the design language, all cloud documents that are subscribed to the source of truth receive updates. Other designers can preview and accept these – keeping everyone in sync."

At the heart of the design system is the component – the atomic element that allows for the creation of more complex units. The components in XD are flexible enough to support the nearly endless contextual customization that users of the design system need to have to build with it.

What about the future?

Helping teams and enterprises create more design consistency and efficiency is an important first step in building a design system, but there are broader, underlying problems that create related challenges in other parts of the workflow. So Adobe will keep talking to customers to learn more about the pain points they're trying to solve with design systems and true to the XD way, finding and addressing the underlying, root causes.

The benefits of a design system align well with what Guzman has in mind: "The real power behind design systems is that it will allow designers to focus on the more central questions: how is this business or service or product that I'm designing bringing value to someone's life? How am I keeping my customers' needs in the center of everything I'm doing?"

"We have a great opportunity in front of us to take what we've learned from executing design systems at scale, and with great complexity, and building some of those lessons into our products and services moving forward." - Shawn Cheris

Part 2

Making it into a success

It's become increasingly clear that a design system needs to be co-created with wide audiences

Building on a deep, human understanding

"Put energy in creating something more meaningful, more delightful, rather than just getting shit done."

– Petri Heiskanen,
SVP of Design, Idean

"You're creating a foundational, underlying system that should align and change people's behavior for hundreds or thousands of people around the world. So yeah, there's nothing easy about that. The key to this is involving the right people, in the right way, at the right time."

–Matias Vaara,
Creative Director, Idean

"We just looked at it as a user-centered design problem, internally. The positive impact on our teams, on our products, and our end users."

– Joseph McLaughlin, Partner, Director of Design, Microsoft

"It's a wake-up call for many. More people have stepped up. There's more awareness of what design can do: not just "hand me the button" but "how do we make it better?"

– J F Grossen, VP of Design, Global, HERE Technologies

Design systems are made for people

Investing in a design system means investing in communication and engaging the whole organization into a broader collaboration.

A design system is an enabler

Introducing a design system requires taking the time to build empathy with those whose lives it's going touch. It's important to understand their day-to-day challenges, processes, and workflows.

It also means communicating the design system's aspiration, intent, benefits, and value, not just to the business as a whole, but to specific groups. It means helping others understand - and experience first hand - how the system helps them get their job done faster. It means nudging their focus and energy to solve higher value problems.

It also means delivering the design system in a way that engages, inspires, and makes it easier to act in the ways we say we'd like to but not always end up doing.

In this aspect, a design system is like any other human-centric design initiative: it takes active collaboration.

A design system should catch on

The core team (or a more distributed team, if that's the case) has a unique responsibility toward the system. They are the ones that apply their craft to create the assets, tools, and guidelines that will bring the shared vision to life, for the benefit of customers and other end users. They won't achieve this feat on their own.

For a business and its customers to enjoy the benefits of an established design system, anyone who influences the outputs (a clue: not just the product organization) needs to be capable and comfortable using the system, be it through the tools and assets, or the shared activities provided.

Tip

What you value might be different from everyone else's

- Keep sitting down with all the immediate, potential users and stakeholders for a chat or demo
- Identify what particular benefit or output would make the design system relevant to them in particular

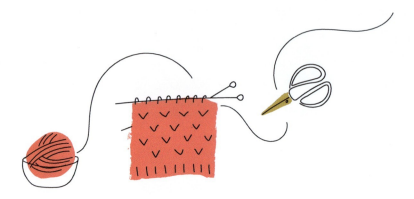

A design system requires structure

Engaging others in a collaborative journey doesn't mean indulging in design by committee. It is possible to combine a strong creative vision and artistic direction by engaging with the community of design system users. The main purpose here is to learn together, to create interest, to drive engagement, and to gain contributions.

This takes place in initial research, visual and pattern exploration, curating and showcasing, as well as outlining and distributing and executing final deliveries for everyone's benefit. Misunderstandings and minor conflicts along the way are guaranteed. After all, we're only human. We are better off taking the time to learn from each other.

> **Tip**
>
> Walk a mile in their shoes, and invite others to walk in yours:
>
> - Stress test the system with a few product teams in the early prototyping phase
> - Embed design system creators in product teams and other units for a little while
> - Invest in regular, social, open door activities

"If someone has a meeting with you to figure out how to get onboard with your design system, then you don't have a design system. You just have some assets that people need to be introduced to."

Jeoff Wilks, Director, Carbon Design System, IBM

Building the mechanisms that keep it alive

"We're pushing forward into a time where the screen is not going to be the only interaction point in UI for our products. And so, thinking about things like voice, like virtual or augmented reality. How are these going to affect our design systems?"

– Jason Cyr, Director,
 Design Transformation, Cisco

"Products are never done. We need to have a team and support in place to continue to iterate based on what we learn from either our users and their feedback, or the direction that technology or the industry are going."

– Nick Cochran, Design Practices Lead, ExxonMobil

"A design system needs to be kept alive and evolving as much as possible. It's not an end game."

– Emanuela Damiani, Senior UX Product Designer, Mozilla

Becoming a part of everyday operations

A design system's success depends on its frequent adoption by the dozens (or hundreds) of products a company has on the market. It has this twofold nature of being a product and serving other products.

The consequence of this is that a design system becomes successful to the extent it fits into the processes and operations of the product teams, with their needs for constant evolution and support. It needs to have a quality and ability to scale that requires much more rigorous workflow than a style guide, and consistent collaboration with different teams. It requires governance and speed.

A living, evolving product

A design system is a living part of the organization. It's not finished after the first version is created. Instead, it follows the needs and evolutions of different products - and most importantly, shifts in the market and customer preferences.

That means your design system is going to cater to a set of needs that require exceptions and versions. Building an understanding of what is shared, how much flexibility there is, what the limitations are, etc. is hard work, but part of the intangible value a design system creates.

The makers of a system are tasked with approaching it with the knowledge that will include history, versions, and in-built flexibility for the components and systematic elements. If not, the design system will turn from a shining initiative full of promise to a burden that lost touch with the reality of the products it's meant to serve.

In the early stages of a design system, it's understandable that there are more changes to be made. It might be hard to define exact timelines. The more mature a design system becomes and the more dependencies there are, the more demand for stability there is.

Adjusting responsibilities and creating new touchpoints for internal collaboration

When first building a design system, it's necessary to start having the styles and components embedded to the live products. This way, product teams can trust the quality and implement the assets quickly in their day-to-day work. Full backlogs and previous prioritizations will then need to be re-negotiated.

Reducing the friction and awkwardness for teams and products that are already running at full speed is essential. It requires time and effort, as it's not only the implementation of the product but also workflows and decision-making practices that need to evolve.

Instead of teams spending time on basic assets, these discussions become part of the design system community. For some teams and individuals, this can be a relief. For others, it's a big leap to take.

Even for teams who are keen to adopt the system, figuring out how to do it in practice can be a challenge. At times, management will need to provide support to keep the roll-out going.

> **Tip**
>
> Introducing a design system means adding new workflows. The design system should be an enabler, so it's essential to understand its impact:
>
> - Do some research on what's holding individuals and teams back in their day-to-day work
> - Map out what individuals and teams need more time on
> - Keep going over the desired behavior changes, helping individuals and teams start forming new practices

Aren't we already working like this?
Sharing code or design assets like this is nothing new. What's new is the scope, making it cross-disciplinary, and the ways to govern it.

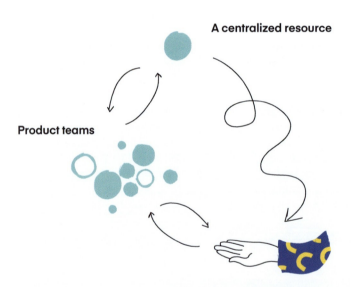

> "We would keep every historical version of the system available until all of our digital products have migrated to an updated version."

Josh Baron, Senior Principal Product Designer, Dell

Understanding the way designers and developers do - or should - work together

The best way to reduce the team's workload and keep the rhythm and pace across various products is to have the system cover both development and design.

It's not a design system without proper mechanisms in place to keep design and development in sync, offering new ways to collaborate and specialize.

The most immediate benefit of having live assets is the ability to demonstrate behaviors - not just to describe them or simulate them. This directly cuts down the time required for creating detailed specs.

It allows the emphasis in handovers to shift to the desired objectives. It also allows for more rapid prototyping, with designers and developers working in parallel rather than within their own, separate environments.

The design system team can then create a series of quality assurance and control procedures to maintain the scalability of the system.

> **Tip**
>
> A design system team can't ignore how a centralized change might affect the product teams:
>
> - Spend enough time understanding the product ecosystem and priorities
> - A strong partnership and continuous communication on the "candidate changes" need to happen before they are put in place
> - Aim for a predictable, regular release intervals
> - Create a definition for what's a breaking change, and how often it can happen

It's not just the assets but the way they are implemented

With basic components and styles implemented more consistently and without the need for custom tweaks, it becomes easier for the teams to always pull in the latest assets. As a result, rolling out UI updates across various instances becomes significantly faster. Not only does this mean that products start to feel more aligned, but it helps to reduce the gap that often exists between "product reality" and the desired state. At least, this is the case when the implementation and workflows have been developed with this particular model in mind. It's great to set ambitious goals, but it would be naive to expect changes to take place overnight.

For some design systems, a strong union of products and centralized resources might not even be the right goal. In these cases, the emphasis is put on doubling the efforts on the shared principles and overarching philosophy. Potential duplication of work across teams is seen as less of a concern. In shared sessions, highly autonomous teams come together to share inspiration and success stories. Again, the decision between these two models (and every variation in-between and besides them) is best made intentionally, making it possible to steer the system in the right direction.

> **Tip**
>
> A design system won't provide all the answers. Finding boundaries is essential to set the right expectations:
>
> - Find a clear answer to what the system needs to deliver - and what remains a responsibility
> - Often, a design operations specialist, a service designer, or a business analyst is required to evolve the processes
> - Close collaboration with a tech lead, or architect, can both define the needs of current production and pave the way for its evolution

Taking product portfolio management into account

It's easy to assume that a design system should apply 100% to everything an organization produces. After all, this would provide maximum uniformity and efficiency. In practice, this often proves impossible. It also begs the questions of what exactly "being aligned with the system" means. It's essential to understand both the current and future offerings. By helping to invest more time into the system wisely, it will provide an invaluable toolkit for roll-out and adoption-related negotiations.

Making it relevant for broader audiences

As a rule of thumb, the overarching philosophy and principles apply to everything. So does the possibility to share relevant insights. Each existing unit, product, and individual within an organization is likely to have a various set of definitions of what truly matters going forward. Mapping these out will bring the differences and the commonalities to light. These are the critical priorities, key messages and mindsets that resonate across the organization.

The underlying foundations are also aligned not only with the particular units most heavily using the system but to a broader context and dependencies that are taken into account. The design system is unlikely to be the only changed initiative around, and there will be units and teams who are heavily invested in their current approach and implementation.

Finding "north star" statements (as well as great examples of their expression in practice) gives the design system a purpose. It also makes it more likely that the design system is going to survive as soon as the sparring on the tangible, hands-on tools and assets begins. The better the reasons for making changes, the more efforts can be put into it. The better the design system matches the needs of a team or unit going forward, the easier it is to adopt.

Finding the right approach for each
The more widely used and the more future-proof something is, the sooner it needs to be considered by the design system. In particular, this applies to the UI foundations, service patterns, supported frameworks and platforms, tools, specific UI assets, and variants, or any other outputs that are tied to a particular medium. This way, what is provided by the system fits the needs for most, if not all, teams leveraging the system in their daily work. In practice, there will be a good deal more considerations at play other than current adoption and expected lifecycle, including the definition of "sufficient alignment." For example, in the early stages of a design system, running a pilot with early adopters and champions, wherever those might be found, can bridge the way to the business critical cases. With adoption well underway, demands for the design system might grow faster than the rate at which high quality, validated assets can fit well together and have a clear purpose to be reasonably produced.
Over time, there will be a need to depreciate and kill some aspects that were supported before.

Thrown into all of this is the selected governance approach, i.e., a highly distributed vs. centralized, and curation for various aspects of the system, i.e., strict vs. loose rules, and the complexity of the system architecture, i.e., managed as one vs. managed as multiple tiers and sub-extensions. In short, it's likely that there will always be several items on the fringe of a design system's scope. Without a good understanding of the offering and its drivers for the next years, it's harder to know what to push for, and what to say no to.

Understanding where the world is going
Unfortunately, it's rare to find offering-related insights compiled in a way that is immediately applicable to make the design system work. It's much more likely that a good deal of collecting, research, and co-creation are required throughout a design system initiative, both to gain a sense of where the relevant sources are, as well as to make the key takeaways for the design system visible.

In some cases, it's hard to gain support for this kind of preparatory work or to find sufficient bandwidth once the system initiative is already going on. Even then, such discussions tend to bring to light an assumed scope and priorities: Who is the system intended for? Who - and to what extent - will depend on it?

Some of the answers can easily be explored and tested out. However, the bigger the initiative is aiming to be, the more it depends on making smart, sustainable choices.

Tip

Make the scope of the design system both clear and up for debate.

- It helps to have a strong, grounded vision of priorities
- Even if the design system does not support something in terms of assets, it's good to keep raising awareness of the thinking behind a system
- Not everything needs to be aligned the same way (but make the differences and their implications clear)
- It's natural for the scope to evolve over time

Tip

Make sure there are 1-2 people involved in the design system initiative who can run these types of discussions and research

Tip

Keep tabs on how the product/service offering is evolving. In particular, look out for the underlying drivers:

- Start researching from day 1; invest in a more in-depth, 360° mapping early on if you can
- Find ways to map your data and hunches; this makes it easier to iterate on the potential conclusions for the design system
- Be considerate of the granularity level you are going for, i.e. "mountain-top" vs. "bird's-eye view"
- Pick a suitable interval at which you are going to review these key steering materials, discuss whether you're still on track
- Use the maps in your communication, both to raise awareness, and to invite others to share their insights

Ensuring that assets can be implemented into live products

"A design system is a marriage of design and development."

– Josh Baron, Senior Principal Product Designer, Dell

"Using code to help control implementation has been really important."

– David Kendall, Principal, UX Design, AT&T

"Introducing a design system could be introducing change for a lot of people. Not only for the design organization, but the engineering organization, and potentially the product management organization."

– Jeoff Wilks, Director, Carbon Design System, IBM

Collecting a 360° inventory over time

Mountain-top view

- How many brands are there? What's their relationship with each other?
- What focus areas and targets does the latest strategy set? What are the critical categories?
- How is the market changing?
- What's growing, what's dying?
- Which future technologies are already being investigated for potential adoption?
- What capabilities are being invested in? Are there any major organizational changes coming up?

Bird's-eye view

- What makes or breaks the experience for customers? What do they value?
- What makes the brand recognizable? What are some of the best instances where this has been expressed?
- Which services and products tend to go together? What purposes do these serve?
- What are the recurring service patterns across different instances/touchpoints? What's the underlying architecture like?
- Which development framework /design tools are used? What would be the best ways to host assets and code for teams to be able to access and utilize them efficiently?

Badger's-eye view

- What are the key, shared, defining details, and characteristics? What variants/flavors of these exist?
- What are the critical conversion points? Where's the most traffic?
- What are the recurring journey stages / use cases / jobs-to-be-done / user needs?
- Which assets and styles are used most often? Which are most asked for?
- How many teams/units are there? What are their objectives and painpoints?

Mapping where the desired level of "alignment" to a design system lands:

Soulmates	Friends	Distant cousins	Different planets
A change in one is immediately/soon visible in the other.	It's easy for a team to implement updates in the format provided by the system	It matches (some of) the shared principles, and it might even appear the same at first glance, but it's a replica maintained by the team on their own	It has little in common in terms of shared principles and implementation

Steering the roll-out of a design system

"Part of the lead work is to figure out how product teams can adopt this without losing track of their ongoing work."

– Elisa Pyrhönen,
Senior Service Designer, Idean

"Right now, we have components which are robustly designed and developed only for the web part. Our next step is to also have the native mobile components for iOS and Android."

– Marie Petit, Leader of the UX Chapter,
Crédit Agricole Technologies & Services

"When an identity hasn't been thought of from a system perspective in a good digital way, we've had to rethink the identity without breaking it."

– Jules Mahé,
Lead UI Designer, Idean

"We have created a white label, master design system at the bottom. Then on top of it, each product family can have an extension library."

– Robin Klein Schiphorst,
Design Lead, Idean

Keeping it relevant over time

"How will we maintain the system after it's built? How will we prepare our community when the system changes? If teams don't ask those long term questions before they start building, the system will only have one life cycle before it becomes outdated."

– Hayley Hughes,
Design Lead, Airbnb

"It's a cross-functional effort. Because a design system belongs to everyone in the organization, everyone will be able to improve it — if needed."

– Emanuela Damiani,
Senior UX Product Designer, Mozilla

"The critical piece here is - what's the governance: what is the methodology for product managers, or product teams, or product team designers to evolve the system further?"

– Sampo Jalasto,
Head of Design, Idean

Learning to handle incoming contributions

There are two brutal ends in store for design systems that fail to evolve: they are never adopted widely enough, or they go stale over time. To prevent this from happening, there are many decisions to make about the nature of the design system.

There's a new process in town

Introducing a design system means that some decisions that were previously handled by the teams on their own will now be taken care of centrally.

Some individuals and teams will be overjoyed. Others might be less so. In either case, it will take some time and repetitions to get in place and to get it right.

It might be a core team or an extended collective that is governing the design system. In either case, the current checks and balances tend to evolve.

What this decision influences, however, are the ideal means for handling incoming contributions.

How and when do we...?

If the process is not fair, or transparent enough, why should people trust it? After all, they are experts in their own right. If it doesn't feel fast enough, who is accountable for it? After all, people have their deliverables to think of. If another unit owns it and we have no say about it? All of these question present potential pitfalls.

The process model you have in mind for contributions is only as good as it runs in reality. This means being able to:
- Efficiently communicate (and in a way, agree on) when and how individuals, teams, and other units can and should become involved
- Have a feasible way of handling all of this in a way that works for all involved
- Make sure that the design system evolves based on contributions, but also provides sufficient stability for the units and teams it serves

To set expectations, it would also help to set some clear decisions on:
- What platforms, products, channels, etc. does the design system (currently) need to support?
- What's the steering group that can both follow up on the progress of the design system, as well as provide support in issues that need to be escalated?

Tip
- Should you have a core team or extended collective nurturing the design system? We believe that in most cases, it's best to have the best of both worlds
- To make it easier for the teams, build at least partly on the existing tools and workflows that people tend to be familiar with
- Whenever you state a strict rule, whether it's in the documentation or during a session, follow it up with a justification. This helps to keep it transparent: often the underlying reasons are just as relevant to be aware of

Why do we...?

Thinking of the design system as a sign-off procedure doesn't properly capture its potential. A design system is there to help uncover and root down the best practices, ranging from overarching principles practiced each day, to helping specialists come up with answers to very detailed, specific questions. Often, there are no single, right, or wrong interpretations, but a range of options available.

In some ways, having fewer questions is not the objective. Having a proper forum for all the possible interpretations is better and being able to state the latest official, updated versions.

The more people we want to include, the broader the perspectives, backgrounds, and narratives.

And the harder this becomes, the more unique a platform design system can be.

Tip

How many pleasant and helpful things do you think of when you hear the word "process"? Unless your ears just perked up and shoulders went down, you might have memories of the worst bureaucracies. Let's try to steer away from that right away:

- "What if contributing to the system was like going your favorite coffee shop?"

Tip

Before diving into detailed process practices, take a step back, bring people together, and ask:

- When do we need strict rules?
- When do we need loose rules?
- As a whole, where do we land on this continuum, which of these should characterize our design system?

What's the setting?

A place for peer support
No need to keep it formal all the time. Many of the questions and early stage ideas are best handled in a more casual setting:

- Pick a channel for quick questions and casual conversations related to the design system
- Organize face-to-face sessions, open door days, training sessions, casual meetups, etc. to bring individuals from different units and teams together
- When sparring with an individual or specific team, discuss what the purpose of the session is (e.g., mutual learning vs. a formal review)

- If you are not seeing any contributions coming in through your formal process(es), some tweaks and changes are needed
- If you're recognizing too many contributions coming in at once, it's a definite problem, but still, one you need to address and openly communicate about

The formal process
Having a proper structure for incoming requests takes a lot of the stress and hassle away, especially when times are busy:

- Automate what you can to make it easier to keep track of both the individual requests, as well as the overarching trends
- You want to benefit from a wide range of inputs, not just the loudest voices

What's the difference between loose and strict rules?

Loose rules

- Emphasis on **recommendations**
- Documentation can be more limited and **open ended**
- Updates to the shared assets can be more **organic**
- Teams have more freedom and **autonomy** to explore what goes into (and out of) the system

---

What are the risks to watch out for?

Loose rules

- **Uncertainty**; feeling that the design system and its assets do not provide sufficient answers
- Confusing creative freedom with a permission to be **sloppy and inconsistent**
- **The teams preferring to keep producing custom tweaks to even the basic assets**, keeping up the design and development debts
- Dropping the design system as **"nobody uses it anyways"**

Strict rules

- Emphasis on **requirements**
- Documentation tends to be more **precise and exhaustive**
- Updates to the shared assets need to go through a strict **review and distribution processes**
- Various mechanisms are in place to ensure **compliance and trust** in the decisions made within the system

---

Strict rules

- **Fear and censorship**; feeling that experimentation is frowned upon and suggestions are likely to be shot down
- **Preserve ineffective or outdated patterns** as well as the good ones
- **The teams' focus slipping to reviews and checks** rather than the customer and business needs (especially when the design system checks are not the only ones around)
- Dropping the design system as it becomes **too limiting**

Which one should we go for?

Loose rules
- There's an underlying need to **evolve the offering**; the target audiences, contexts of use, business rules are changing significantly
- **UI assets that have not (yet) been made part of the system** can be created (preferably keeping the shared principles and UI foundations in mind)

How important is it?

On a higher level
To establish the boundaries of

- The underlying principles should be in constant use but revised rarely, e.g., once each year (unless there's a significant shift in markets/customers/ brand
- The underlying UI foundations should be as future-proof as possible while supporting existing, major platforms/ products that have a life expectancy of x amount of years
- The UI assets evolve as new insights are gained or as the defining principles/ foundations are changed

Strict rules
- There's an underlying need to **stabilize the offering**; the various target audiences, contexts of use, business rules, etc. have become fairly established
- **Core brand assets** tend to always follow strict rules. **Principles** and **UI foundations** tend to ensure that assets go well together, meaning that these definitions tend to benefit from being more robust.

On a tactical level
When in doubt, use these two questions to determine whether it should become, or stay a part of the system

- Would it be of high functional/emotional value to end users?
- Would it be used by multiple/all teams?

Expert tips on scaling the design system

> *"Have a shared vision and do not hesitate to change things if you see that you are not on the right path."*
>
> – Audrey Hacq,
> Design Lead, Idean

> *"I wish that we had set up some more usability tests or feedback sessions along the way that got into the details of the implementation. Not just the philosophy and the concepts, but the implementation choices made for code and UX design."*
>
> – Nick Cochran, Design Practices Lead, ExxonMobil

> "It's imperative to keep the momentum going, to keep people engaged, keep people excited."
>
> – J F Grossen, VP of Design, Global, HERE Technologies

> "We hosted these two-day design jams. And they were a great success for several reasons like for culture, for sharing, collaboration. But more importantly, it allowed all of our creative teams to stress test the new design system."
>
> – David Kendall, Principal, UX Design, AT&T

Scaling with pilots, building in feedback loops

A design system is like any other product: Building it in isolation reduces the likelihoods of success.

Why is it essential to involve internal users?
The best way to lower the threshold for adoption is to ensure that internal users, ("makers" leveraging the system) are part of the development process.Ultimately, it's about their everyday work. And to take action, it's good to know why something is done the way it is - otherwise, it seems to lack purpose and direction. Being part of it earlier on also makes it all easier to absorb. There are fewer unknowns. As for the design system curators, engaging with the various makers helps gain an understanding for what will work and what will not: what is feasible with current processes, which parts should be open to change, and which should remain as they are. It's also an opportunity to raise awareness, and to spot where potential misunderstandings are stemming from.

Why is it essential to involve end users and customers?
A design system serves to make internal processes smoother and more effective, but the real end user is the customer - people who will be interacting with the company's brand and products.
It's likely that a good deal of a design system initiative's efforts goes towards making it the best for internal teams working on brand, development, and design. However, per the definition of brand perception, user experience, and customer experience, they can never be forced - they can only be facilitated. Therefore, it's essential for a design system - both the curators and the makers - to stay focused on the "external" insights.

Making it into a success

The 3-3-3 test

Running this exercise will provide you with a prioritized shortlist of up to 9 screens and 27 components to test your design system with.

Goal

Provide a view of what future products and services will look and feel like. Validate your principles and shared assets.

Steps

1. Do a mapping of your whole company's products and components as part of the inventory.
2. Identify three critical products or product families if you have a large organization.
3. From each of these three products or product families, you choose three key, critical screens.
4. Select three critical components from these selected screens.
5. You now have a prioritized shortlist of screens and components to start your test with.
6. Make two versions: a safe one and a bold one. The safe version aims for steady improvements. The bolder version can go a little bit overboard, showcasing what an ideal, super solution might look and feel like.

> **Tip**
>
> Focus on what matters:
>
> - Focus on the signature moments that make or break the experience for end users. These are the instances when love (or hate) sparks for the product or brand. These may or may not be the same across different products and services
> - Focus on a holistic UI, even if it's a snapshot: the interactions, the motion, the semantic structure, the responsiveness, etc. Otherwise, it can too easily be seen as "just a bit prettier than before"

> **Tip**
>
> Why not make it a joint effort?
>
> - Run interviews and workshops to get to a deeper understanding of the portfolio and business logic
> - Invite representatives of the teams responsible for the products and services for a day, or even just half a day, to be part of the explorations

Follow up with one of these activities:

- Review what you learned about these "must win" cases.
- Share the result of the explorations.

Communicating it well, time and time again

"As a part of the Fluent Design System, we've set up a Fluent learning series, where we're bringing people in to learn about different tools, different processes, different design areas, like accessibility. It's a learning series. It's broad, and there are design talks, there are tooling talks, there's a lot of different ways to engage via online or in person and we're looking at what people are responding to there. That's helping us understand what's of value and how to prioritize the things that are seeming of value, as well."

– Joseph McLaughlin, Partner, Director of Design, Microsoft

"The more you talk about it, the easier it becomes. Involve the right and even the wrong people."

– Karolina Boremalm,
  Managing UX Designer, Idean

"Having heard somebody else say something about it and having experienced it first hand, those are two completely different things."

– Elisa Pyrhönen,
  Senior Service Designer, Idean

"Make sure everyone is in the loop and understands what has been done, clarify the choices you've made, as well as why you've made those decisions."

– Audrey Hacq,
  Design Lead, Idean

Communication is a deal-breaker

Whether it's the nature of larger companies in particular, or the wide-reaching nature of design systems (both, we suspect), through our industry reviews, we've found that communication was repeatedly mentioned as a critical activity.

A design system's channels ranges from documentation to in-person activities. The quality of these determines whether people are both able and willing to apply shared guidance in their day-to-day decision making.

There is a clear overlap here to the way the design system is delivered, and the way contributions are taken in. In this chapter, however, we'll be focusing on awareness raising in particular, as the need for it never completely shifts away.

Understanding the existing culture and practices

The tactics for effective communication vary depending on company's size, structure, culture, and design maturity level. Some companies quickly accept, adapt, and incorporate a design system into their work processes. They have an entrepreneurial mindset and are often interested in trying new methods to gain an advantage over their competitors. However, they are also the ones most prone to abandon the design system once "the next big thing" catches their eye. Without a proper model to scale various, early-stage experiments to more established initiatives, the resources required to keep the design system up and running will eventually run out.

Companies that are more hierarchical in their structures can be more difficult to convince about the pros of a design system. The inevitable ambiguity during the early learning stages and first pilots can feel unusual, even uncomfortable. Approaching other units and decision makers requires a more formal approach. And so implementing a design system in companies like these often mean securing initial buy-in from top management for funds and resources, at the same time as winning over and empowering teams on lower levels to promote the required changes to implement a design system.

Finding the right communication practices

Finding the right communication practices is part of the design system creation process. In the early stages, the focus of communication is on raising awareness and creating chances to get an official blessing or an initial investment.

As the design system development starts to roll out, many of the needed communication patterns are realized and established. While working with early adopters and a wider test audience, you come across questions like:

- What is it for?
- How should it be used?
- What works for us, and what doesn't?

As the design system evolves, the need for information about how to govern it, use it, and expand it, is just as strong as the initial phase. The difference is that there's an even greater variety of audiences, both in terms of interests and awareness levels. And so with this evolution, more teams are dependent on the updates.

To meet the needs of the growing audiences and channels, the means of communication need to be clear and well functioning.

For the core team, this means finding ways to standardize at least some of their communication practices, whether it's in the form of training sessions, workshops, meetups, reviews, shared selection criteria, an online learning resource, release notes, or something else entirely.

Tip

Find the right channels and sessions to continue raising awareness:

- Make the most of existing communication channels and meetups
- Introduce regular activities that the core team or system champions can run
- Allocate enough time for the team to create and maintain communication and documentation materials
- Enable other sources of information, e.g., leads, key units, who can tell the story and promote the system as well

Tip

Find your elevator pitch:

- Find a short, memorable way to introduce the design system
- Follow up the intro with a question, e.g., "How does that sound to you?"
- This helps shift it from a one-sided pitch to a discussion and mutual learning opportunity

Tip

Work across company layers for a stronger, cross-organizational understanding:

- Top-level executives need to be convinced of the value and objectives of the design system, but they are rarely aware of (or extensively interested in) the difficulties in practicalities that their subordinates are facing
- The makers who will adopt the system have their day-to-day jobs to think about. Running onboarding sessions and participatory workshops help build good working knowledge on the new practices over time

> **Tip**
>
> Build a human connection. It's not just more helpful, but often the most effective way to communicate:
>
> - If you can't meet in person, make a video call to build the human connection
> - If it's a really big team, communication might be harder. In this case, run it with the leads and enable them to pass it on in person to the rest of their teams

> **Tip**
>
> Set up a steering committee to ensure the continued management and sponsorship for the design system initiative:
>
> - Provide both qualitative and quantitative updates on the progress and impact of the design system
> - A design system isn't a standard product: it can take management some time to learn how to best support and provide steering input for it

> **Tip**
>
> Communication isn't a one-way street. It's essential that other questions, comments, and concerns are heard:
>
> - Listen and look for who might be interested and who is too quiet
> - Sometimes, instead of answering a question, it's good to respond with "What do you think? I'd like to hear your point of view"

"We had the chance to have enough time (almost two months) to carry out a real framing phase, to research and prioritize. This crucial step also allowed us to convince the internal management to unlock the budgets, and to co-create with the stakeholders the end-game vision of the design system."

Audrey Hacq, Design Lead, Idean

The types of communication and activities that keep it flowing

Who	Why
Makers - internal employees, vendors, partners, customers' teams, etc. those leveraging the system	• Gaining a good working knowledge on the design system and its objectives. • The feedback given and questions raised help see what works and what doesn't
Stakeholders - management, key units, partners, etc.	• Awareness that it exists, and why it exists • Providing support for the initiative as needed • Actively inviting other companies to build on the same platform
Broader public	• Public relations for potential employees
End users (customers, employees)	• Understanding the gap between internal definitions and end users reality

Where	How
• An easy-to-access, online learning resource (the design system site) • Blog and social media • Bootcamp • Demo sessions • Discipline / unit specific meetups • Facilitated workshops • Internal communication channels • Monthly newsletter • Regular, system specific meetups • Team's own reviews and sign-offs • Steering meetings • The tools used to deliver / leverage the system and its assets • Webinars • Industry awards	• Do's and don'ts • Frequently asked questions • Hands-on exercises • Key definitions and mantras • Latest updates and release notes • Live previews • Panel discussions • Practical, illustrative examples • Short video(s) • Success stories • Talks • Templates
• Conferences and industry specific meetups • Hiring funnel	
• Regular user tests, observation, interviews, field visits • Analytics reviews, A/B and multi-variate tests, surveys, minipolls • Reports and review sessions	• Key takeaways • Statistics • Video summaries • Quotes

Rethinking what "communication" means

Let's face it, training and communication can sound a bit boring.

Goal

Raising a design system's awareness with engaging activities can be effective.

Steps

1. Gather a group of people together.
2. Go through the following questions as a warm-up, one by one:
3. What did it feel like when you first learned to swim, to ride a bike? What did it feel like when you had an "aha" moment?
4. How would you teach that skill or idea to somebody else most effectively?
5. How would you prefer to learn more about it?
6. If you were handed a package to do that, what would convince you that it really works for you?
7. After sharing your experiences, shift towards considering how these might best be applied when it comes to the design system.

> **Tip**
> - You can use a paper canvas if you'd like. Find a suitable room and place each warm-up question on a stretch of wall
> - Getting people up and moving not only provides a break from sitting at a desk, it subtly changes the dynamics of discussion and ideation

Follow up with one of these activities:

- Turn your learnings into to-dos to get it implemented.
- When running your communication activities, keep actively inviting feedback on what works and what doesn't.

a	
b	
c	
d	

Nick Cochran,
Design Practices
Lead, ExxonMobil

Nick Cochran, ExxonMobil on the importance of communication

"I would recommend making communication and collaboration a full-time role for someone as you are developing and rolling out a design system. That was my main role during the project. I wasn't putting my hands on code or pushing pixels. I was reviewing some of the work that was done and helping to provide direction. My role was also being the interface to the organization, the champion to share and communicate. That is a crucial role in any successful design system implementation.

My job was to help address concerns and to make sure the organization felt heard and that they had the avenue to collaborate. Not everybody wants to, but for the ones who did, we wanted to make it very clear that they could play an active role in the project. It is so essential for any design system project to commit serious time and resources to this communication and collaboration aspects of the effort.

One thing that we did was not rely enough on our one big round of upfront interviews with our users of the design system. We did our research at the beginning when we kicked the project off. It was great—we were able to hear from a lot of these designers, developers, and other stakeholders at the start of the project through these typical user research interviews. That helped us shape the direction from the start. Based on these learnings, we were able to set the principles for the system. It also helped people from the beginning to feel heard and connected to the work.

Though we didn't stop communicating with these people after that, what we didn't do, and I wish we had done, was to bring some of these same people back in to do what would amount to a usability test or something that was like testing a prototype of the design system. Our project team had been making choices as we created the design system, the component library, and the designs that backed it up. Implementation choices were being made like using flexible layouts instead of rigid grids. Some of those choices were new to people, and I wish we had the chance to engage in those discussions and hear feedback from our designers and developers sooner."

It's a custom solution that fits your organization

Many of the more widely-known design systems are open to the public. Or to be a bit more specific, the design system sites, blogs, and conference talks on these systems are easy to find.

This makes it possible to explore alternatives, benchmarking how others have solved specific aspects of their system. But no matter how good their design system is, it will not fully fit the needs of your company. Each design system is unique.

Culture fit

Each organization has its unique flavor. Understanding this differentiating identity before starting on the design system specifics helps guide the decisions in the right direction.

It's alright to have different teams and units with their own, specific flavor. It can even be a sign of active communities within an organization. However, for the design system to be something all these different teams can subscribe to, it's good to find an overarching "truth." The answer to this might reside in the heritage of the organization, a drive for a future vision, or something else entirely.

Process fit

It doesn't make sense to upset the whole set-up. For example, if people are used to discussing through a particular channel or in an existing meetup, why not keep it that way. On the other hand, if a significant share of people find a specific step or internal touchpoint to be a bottleneck, why not suggest a better alternative.

The governance model, in particular, will vary depending on the organization structure and culture, and hence the processes. Ideally, the design system would be owned and positioned in a way that makes it possible to quickly reach out to the teams and units that need to be involved.

> **Tip**
>
> Benchmarking existing, public design system resources is an excellent way to gain a sense of different, potential ways to present a design system. Here are some of the design systems our interviewees have been working on to get you started:
>
> - Airbnb Design Language System
> - Dell Clarity
> - IBM Design Language
> - Microsoft Fluent
> - Adobe Spectrum

> **Tip**
>
> When benchmarking public design system resources, keep in mind that it's harder to gain a view of all the internal activities and decisions keeping the design system going

Technology fit

There will always be several technologies "under the hood." Ideally, a design system will provide framework-independent, future-proof means to build a recognizable, fit-for-purpose experience across the various platforms and touchpoints.
In practice, this requires a solid understanding of the preferred technologies.
In terms of the roll-out, it's necessary to define which technologies will extend to the design system it applies to.

Tip
The more you align with the company's must-win goals, the more successful you will be. • Map out what goals the design system will help your organization, and the individuals within it achieve • Focus on mid-term and long-term objectives in particular

"In many ways, a design system is a universal tool, but it is also unique to each organization."

– David Kendall, Principal, UX Design, AT&T

"A design system needs to fit the organization it serves, but it's also going to change the way things are done."

– Elisa Pyrhönen, Senior Service Designer, Idean

"It's a lot of work up front, to do this. This isn't a one size fits all approach."

– Joseph McLaughlin, Partner, Director of Design, Microsoft

Maintaining design systems

The creation, communication, and maintenance of a design system is an endeavor that goes beyond part contribution, side-job, and best-effort models. It requires a small, dedicated team of craftsmen, storytellers, and facilitators to make and ensure the adoption of a design system. Often, the composition of this core team evolves, alongside the design system.

The larger the organization, and the more products it has, the more this team is fundamental to act as a catalyst rather than as a design system police.

Are there any alternatives to having a core team?

Some companies are able to create and maintain a design system without a dedicated design system team. In these cases, the maintenance of the design system is distributed, relying entirely on contributions from different product teams.

This is sometimes called the federated model. The success of this model is dependent on a mature, full understanding of the benefits of a "common" system. It tends to thrive only in organizations where the incentives do not create biases for selfish behaviors.

In the long-term, we have seen that these fully distributed models tend to crumble or be deprioritized under the pressure of short-term budgetary priorities: the very same that might be an initial barrier to having a dedicated team for it.

Can a team do it on their own?

We've also seen and heard of cases where the design system initiative was started in isolation: a small team launching a hero project of their own.

Being passionate about design systems is great, but not making it into a collaborative effort becomes a pitfall sooner or later. Not having the proper support provided by a well-set initiative also risks system champions burning out, without ever reaching the satisfaction and quality of work to be expected.

Even in the cases where there is a perfect set up, team and support models, the design system team needs to be willing to engage with others.

Establish partnerships and collaborations
Not all the work needs to be done by the core team. Trying to do this is not sustainable.

The core team is responsible for driving the vision, core aspects, and the evolution of the design system, and establishing the partnerships and collaborations that ensure the system is fit-to-purpose, implemented, and evolving.

Opening up the design system to a larger group of advocates and collaborators can feel daunting. In the long run, however, this has proven as the most successful approach. Feeling involved and having a good working knowledge of the design system ensures not just higher adoption: it means that the skills of applying and maintaining the system become more widely spread within the organization.

Key roles and targets for engagement

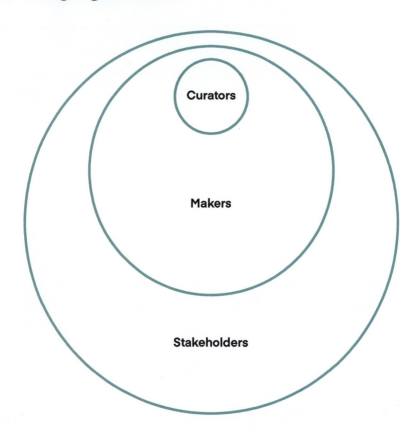

Curators
- Lead the system initiative and set the vision
- Curate what goes in and out of the system
- Actively involve others

Makers
- Primary users of the system to create product and services
- Central knowledge from a shared library for those who use the assets and tools provided by the system on a day-to-day basis in their work
- High awareness for those involved in the reviews and work prioritization of these individuals and teams
- High awareness for all on the shared philosophy, principles, and processes related to the system

Stakeholders
- Benchmark awareness of the initiative and its objectives
- Bringing in more perspectives and insights
- Supporting the initiative as needed

Customers and end users
- People interacting with the brand through product and service experiences

Who should be on our core team?

☐ Product perspective

☐ Marvelous crafts(wo)men

☐ Amazing engineering

☐ End user enthusiasm

☐ Great communication

☐ Super facilitation and networking skills

☐ Senior-level oversight and vision

☐ Other, _____

Start with a couple of experienced craft(wo)men to make sure every design choice brings value, distinctiveness, and coherence; ideally one of the two with a strong technical background - so that the design system can start living in code soon. Systemic thinking and re-usability of work is a must, as it will allow others to leverage the system in their own work and deliverables.

One or more people needs to have keen human-centric design expertise. This ensures that what goes into the system serves those using it, and end users and customers. The ability to leverage analytics is a plus.

Add a storyteller: a person who's going to be able to communicate the reasons why a design system is essential, and create the narrative (and the artifacts) to persuade management, product managers, designers, developers, and others of the importance of its adoption.

Also, add a person who can build the design system's governance model. S/he might be a service designer, or coming from the DesignOps team, or be a product owner. It's important to have this perspective from the beginning, as facilitating these discussions and prototyping the processes significantly reduce uncertainty around what the design system might mean for everyday work.

A design system needs a product owner. S/he is the one who, together with the team, sets the horizon of the work, defines objectives, measures the success of the system. Strong collaboration and networking skills are a must as s/he communicates with top management, product teams, product managers, and other units. S/he is also someone working with the key stakeholders to push for adoption and protect the core team's skills and focus on the key priorities.

It's also essential to plan for the growth of the team, or at least for the temporary contribution from other specialists. Architects, copywriters, photographers, illustrators, or motion specialists are not necessarily part of the core team from the beginning, but they will become increasingly critical as your design system evolves.

Supporting the curators

> **Tip**
>
> Whether your design system initiative starts as a top-down decision, or as a bottom-up effort by a few champions, begin building a community of advocates. Get people to experience it first hand. Having more people with a sense of the overarching philosophy and fundamental mechanisms helps to make the system more stable over time

> **Tip**
>
> You might be lucky if your team can fill two (or even three) roles. However, even the most unicorn and versatile person deserves people that can help them. It's not only more helpful: it also reduces the risk of shouldering it all, instead of actively engaging others in work

> **Tip**
>
> A small organization (or a little initiative within a large organization) can get started with open-sourced references and tools, reducing the need to craft everything from scratch. Getting started and gaining the first results will pave the way for the next steps

How might we best collaborate with different teams in the product organization?

Having designers, developers, and their key stakeholders onboard from day one is key. Without them, the system won't be effective. Use the first few weeks (or months) to experiment with different partnership models. We've collected a few examples here to get you started:

Pass-the-ball

The design system team works on a few examples of work that another team (or unit) takes as a reference and adapts to make them useful for a variety of use-cases.

The design systems team can then take the work done and finalize the reference to include in the design system. As these are released, the collaborating teams implement the latest, "official" versions.

Pilot

The design system team works closely with a small set of products. For a time, the boundaries of the various teams (and their stakeholders), or at least a specific team, and the design system team become blurred.

As a result, the work done is a foundation for a more extensive design system, or the updated system is released to the next set of audiences.

Sparring

This is the loosest form of collaboration, where a design system team acts as a feedback-giver to a product design team, and help them define the design by asking questions, providing feedback and recommendations.

This form of collaboration is especially suited when a team is working on something that should be included in the system but isn't yet official.

Centrica

Industry:
Energy & Services

Employees:
30k

Headquarters:
United Kingdom

Design system implementation:
8-9 months and ongoing

Creating awesome experiences for millions of customers

Working with the UK's largest energy supplier to build a design system that unites their business and allows us to create coherent, engaging experiences for their customers.

Success Story - Centrica

"From the very beginning, this was an amazing collaboration across lots of different departments and skill sets, with executive buy-in from our Centrica Group Chief Marketing Office Marg Jobling. I believe that this is truly a turning point in how design is recognised in our company. It shows how we are evolving with the right ambition to drive us forward in digital."

Paul Roberts, Global Digital Director

Building a new era

British Gas is an established UK brand, owned by Centrica. Along with the major changes taking place in the energy industry and regulatory environment, there is immense pressure to save costs. At the same time, services and new types of offerings are opening avenues for growth. In both areas, being able to respond to changing customer needs is not seen as a nice add-on, but as one of the pillars of Centrica's strategy.

In the past years, significant investments have been made to Centrica's digital capabilities. These investments have shaped their tech landscape, ways of working, and product teams. A combination of autonomy and support processes have helped teams focus on delivery and testing. On the downside, there have been a growing number of inconsistencies in customer-facing solutions.

Evolutions like these require not only evolving the perception of customers but internal employees and partners as well. The more product teams are held back from lingering inefficiencies, the harder it is for Centrica to make changes that go live and evolve in the markets.

Nucleus Design System

- Nucleus was created out of three initiatives: Brand and marketing teams were looking for means to roll out the latest evolution in the brand and visual language.
- Engineering leads were looking for a more lightweight, future-proof, framework agnostic way of building and re-using UI assets.
- At the same time, interest in design systems was increasing.

It soon became apparent that a core team would be needed. While enthusiastic advocates wanted to be part of the initiative and take part in facilitating a design operations workshop, existing commitments were at risk.

Part 2

The adoption journey

Synthesised from four 45min interviews with five designers on their experiences with the design system so far.

Introducing overarching principles and UI foundations

Before diving into producing UI assets, the core team focused on understanding the principles that would guide shared decision making. While the visual language already came with defined principles, two sets more were added: one for user experience, based on the product teams' shared understanding and targets, and one for accessibility, based on web accessibility standards.

It was essential for the team to translate the latest core brand assets and inspirational visualizations into a tangible foundation. Working on the grid, sizing mechanisms, etc. helped ensure that assets and styles worked well.

As British Gas had already established a design operations function, many essential elements such as regular user testing, contextual observations, internal meetups, early stage, and high-level definition templates, as well as method descriptions were already in place.

Streamlined UI asset production

It was clear that any UI asset produced for the system would need to be consumed by the various digital platforms already in use. This meant that web components came first, with many variants to provide additional flexibility. These would then be either imported or translated into the chosen platforms and frameworks.

The benefit of a model like this is that instead of 20+ teams producing and maintaining the same, recurring assets, and replicating them for various environments, a centralized repository is needed. Overall, customer-facing solutions would be leaner in production, with less custom and more standardized assets in place. Product teams would also be able to pull in the latest updates a lot faster.

This repository would also be governed differently, helping prevent the pain points of past, centralized resources. However, custom solutions are discouraged unless embedded into the system for the benefit of all (including end users). It's easiest to see which specific solutions are working across a broader number of instances.

Leading with outcomes

"I'd thought of having a design system team solely focused on building new components and getting them out for other teams. But in the last year, I've seen a shift to this community and adoption side and the team running sessions to upskill and educate teams. It's changing the culture and engagement across different product teams."

– Matthew Gottschalk, Design Operations Manager

Instead of having a fixed project plan, the core team's activities are shaped by the desired outputs, outcomes, rituals, and roadmap. There were four outputs selected for tracking: how customers are benefiting from it, how product teams are able to trust it, reducing waste in internal processes without sacrificing creativity and collaboration, as well as ensuring the continued well-being of the Nucleus team.

Following up on outcomes each month helps to keep focus on what matters:
- It's another means for a busy team to reflect on the successes and potential pitfalls a bit more objectively.
- Knowing both the ups and downs makes it easier for management to offer support as needed.

In addition to shared rituals, continuous discovery always informs the next steps:
- A collaborative workshop on the meaning and potential processes for collaboration, held before the first launch.
- Short, introductory interviews with product owners and their managers to map the roles and needs of the various product teams in light of the upcoming design system.
- Using a day to onboard new team members in-depth on past decisions, as well as for working together to draft the roadmap, metrics, and priorities for work.

- For the initial launch, workshops with 60 participants in total were held.
- To understand how accessibility guidance might be improved, a series of roundtable discussions were run to know when and how issues creep in.
- Running a discovery sprint, including prototyping, end user testing, web analytics, and internal interviews to inform why and how a particular, major, global component might need to be reformed.
- Interviews with designers on their ongoing journey with Nucleus to identify potential gaps and drivers for adoption.
- Blurring the boundaries of product teams and the Nucleus core team to ensure critical, soon-to-come updates based on the shared foundations, reducing tech and design debt.

Not only are these activities helping in increasing adoption and reducing friction to the product teams everyday work. They are ensuring that more and more individuals are having discussions about what good design and development means for British Gas and Centrica, both in terms of business and end-customers.

Having early adopters has also helped the core team evolve Nucleus. It has also enabled new workflows for teams. For example, being able to preview live assets, trying out copy and image variations, has enabled collaboration on minor campaign updates in much faster cycles.

Being open to collaboration also means being open to tough discussions

New workflows are best experienced first-hand. However, this requires product teams to invest some time outside of their existing commitments. Before new cross-team processes become practiced, it's hard to give them a timeline. So it might put existing backlogs and performance metrics at risk. Sometimes, just the idea of that is enough to bring experiments to a grinding halt. If you have two or more objectives that are worthy but seemingly impossible to have at the same time, which one do you go for?

Even champion and early adopters can act in ways that undermine the system. Successes breed new requests. Not every change discussion is a nice and easy one.

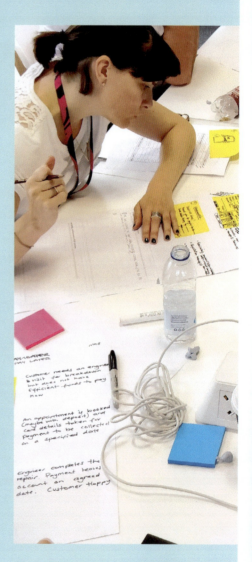

Success Story - Centrica

Conclusion

"Some of our best people are doing some of our best work. We already see the benefits of the design system, but more than that, its influence and reach have been extraordinary. British Gas has provided the rich foundation for wider Centrica adoption from this approach. Super exciting times!"

– Paul Roberts, Global Digital Director

Nucleus has gone live with only a limited set of assets, to a limited set of teams. At the same time, community building has been raised as one of the three key outputs (tools and re-usable UI assets being the other two categories).

Several regular community-building activities are running:
- Nucleus core team members have been participating in meetups of various disciplines and units, both to listen in, and to share updates.
- Catch-ups, feedback sessions and reviews have been run with individuals and teams adopting the assets and styles to better understand how assets are adopted, including potential tweaks and experiments.
- As the community has grown, weekly sessions dedicated to specific, Nucleus-related topics have been introduced.
- A range of discovery tickets have been opened, making it easier for teams to contribute to upcoming assets.
- Testing run by specialist users, in addition to increased awareness early on, ensures that shared UI assets and styles meet accessibility requirements, including but not limited to compatibility with assistive technologies.

3 months in numbers

17%
Quicker page load time, likely to increase as more elements are converted

75+
Participants from different disciplines taking part in weekly Nucleus sessions

42%
More lightweight Nucleus bundle size (kb) (delivered in a way that requires minimal effort from product teams)

20+
Advocates and early adopters who are championing Nucleus

93%
Increase in a browser accessibility score (and encouraging feedback from specialist user tests)

4+
Tough discussions and/or partnerships, working together to adopt Nucleus

10%
Lower bounce rate on an A/B test Nucleus variant

15+
Incoming questions and requests / week to core team members

Part 3

The future of design systems

In a changing landscape, what do we need to start thinking about?

What's your next move?

When we asked our interviewees about the future, many topics came up: the changing nature of our profession, our tools, our organizations, our technologies. Some of the ideas felt radical, but many of these were framed as developments our interviewees have already seen or been expecting in this field for a while.

Instead of definite statements, we used the answers we received to formulate more questions. After all, where's the fun in talking about the future if you're not going to think about your part in it? We've done the introductions. What are your thoughts?

In addition to shared rituals, continuous discovery always informs the next steps:

Over the next few pages, we'll be asking you these questions to get you thinking about the future.

Who are the "product people" of the future?
What are their defining skill sets?

Who cares for craft anymore?
What's a good sign of efficiency?

What role will artificial intelligence play?
What role should we play?

What about service patterns?
What role should APIs and microservices play?

What would be the best design system for voice?
What about gesture-based interfaces?
What about spatial awareness?

What about non-digital experiences?
What about omnichannel experiences?

What's the organization of the future?
What's the ultimate role of a design system?

Who are the "product people" of the future? What are their defining skill sets?

Now that the pixels are done
Let's start with the old news: Our industry has changed. Basic interface patterns and flows for online services have been solved, time and time again. There are different flavors of patterns and styles to choose from, so the pixel-pushing (the mundane work of creating images and graphics) jobs are disappearing.

High fidelity interface design is becoming increasingly accessible with ready-made components and right tooling. Developers and product managers can now do work in a span of a few hours, where it used to take designers many days to complete. While many feel threatened by this, it's a very good thing. It just means that designers do less busywork with mockups, and can focus more time on things that make a difference and have more value like: spending more time with users, exploring alternative solutions, creating new illustrations and brand assets, perfecting service patterns, and thinking beyond the screen.

We're expecting both a few sighs of relief and ultimately, really fascinating things to take place. In the future, we'd like to see more design systems explicitly encourage people to go beyond the UI.

What are your thoughts?

Who cares for craft anymore? What's a good sign of efficiency?

The counter movement
We want to live in a world where creativity and craft continue to prosper even through radical changes. One of the points we've wanted to make in this book is that design systems are not silver bullets. They need to be set up in a way that encourages creativity. Some standardization is good. Too much, and we lose our ability to think for ourselves. We'd like to see more design systems that manage to offer both stability and exploration.

What are your thoughts?

What role will artificial intelligence play? What role should <u>we</u> play?

Better decision-making
We'd like to see a world where algorithms and machine learning help us observe our environment in new ways and challenge our in-built biases. The more rapidly we generate and analyze possible solutions, the more inclusive our models need to be. This way, we can serve more people. The more we make radical personalizations that allow whole designs to be subtly adjusted on the fly, the more mature ethical evaluations we need to make.

After all, we'd like our AI to be not only "intelligent" but also "kind." It's up to us to identify all the surprising forms and patterns these definitions might take.

What are your thoughts?

What about service patterns?

Step up the game
Service patterns are recurring interactions or sets of interactions in a digital product or service. Common service patterns are used to help you: to join or onboard the service, use the service, and leave the service.

Well-designed service patterns encourage users to return to services because of their easy interactions.

Why service patterns are the next iteration of your design system:
- Most of your digital products are services, so being consistent with buttons and layouts is only the first step of creating your design system

- Service patterns make your complex cross-channel services more accessible for customers to navigate and easier for your teams to deliver

- Great services include common interaction patterns or building blocks of common sets of activities, and these patterns should be designed to feel consistent, regardless of the channel it is comes from

- It takes a lot of work to create seamless, consistent front-end experiences, but creating service patterns can make it easier for your tech, systems, and process teams to help you deliver

- Creating common service patterns makes it easier for you to measure success across instances of the patterns

What are your thoughts?

What would be the best design system for voice? What about gesture-based interfaces? What about spatial awareness?

New realities mean fresh design opportunities for designers
It's not just about screens anymore. New modalities like voice, gestural, spatial interactions, as well as virtual- (VR), augmented-(AR), and mixed reality (MR) are becoming increasingly relevant – both for consumer and enterprise use cases. We need to solve things like operating machines with gestures and voice, wayfinding with augmented reality glasses, and how to best handle virtual reality conferencing.

Isn't it about time we saw more public, best-practice setting, design systems in these exciting areas?

The point is all these new modalities are breaking past the boundaries of our focus on screens.

If you're hands-on with products, it's time to start prototyping for voice, gestures, and VR/AR/MR. It's about time that we designers step beyond screens and start shaping how people interact with this brave new world.

What are your thoughts?

What about non-digital experiences? What about omnichannel experiences?

Break more silos
We've seen the digital capabilities of organizations mature over the past years. Major initiatives like these are also one of the reasons why design systems have been in demand.

In the future, it's about time we bridged the gap between digital and non-digital experiences.

This means breaking the remaining silos between different disciplines and units. It means having a better, overarching understanding of the various customer journeys.

If you have a design system in place, it might serve as a great, cross-organizational platform. If you don't yet have a design system in place, be aware that these aspects might not be discussed prominently enough by design system specialists today.

The future of design systems

What are your thoughts?

What's the organization of the future?

Open design systems to wider audiences
We'd like to see more design systems set up with the specific job of serving as enablers, of spotting gaps in the workflows, bringing teams and other disciplines together, and raising questions from all the provided different flavors of customer and user experiences. It can only happen if more people are open to collaboration towards wider audiences.

In the future, maybe we'll need another term to describe culture and collaboration focused initiatives. As the organizational structure and connection points evolve, a design system needs to evolve as well.

What are your thoughts?

Ingredients for success

We've found that each design system initiative would benefit from having these four ingredients taken into account

- Vision and principles
- Shared practices and tools
- Communication and training
- Governance

Our recipe

We hope you've enjoyed this book. The benefit of running hours and hours of interviews means there's an abundance of findings to share. As we've learned, each design system needs to fit the organization in question, but it's also going to change the way things are done. It's a native solution that builds on the brand, culture, maturity, organizational structure, ways of working, desired direction, and audiences to be involved. There have also been clear overlaps and similarities across the different cases we've heard.

As a final step, we'd like to share our synthesis: the Idean recipe for design systems. Instead of a fixed process, we've stated it as the four key ingredients that need to be taken into account in any design system initiative.

Part 3

198

Idean recipe for design systems

Vision and principles

Businesses, products, and services are continually evolving. One of the highlights of a successful design system is being able to express underlying priorities. What principles do we use in our decision making? What is the desired customer experience like? What makes a solution a good fit for your organization? Which of our components and styles reflect this best? This way, product teams are able to explore alternative solutions while keeping shared success criterias in mind.

Shared practices and tools

High-level statements are essential for alignment, but they also need to be applied in practice. A design system needs to be created and delivered in a way that empowers product teams in their everyday work.

Communication and training

Adopting new ways of working takes time and practice, even when the benefits are well understood. Clear communication, demos, and workshops build familiarity early on. They also allow us to listen to the intended users of the system and find the best solutions together. As the design system matures, communication and training provide an essential social aspect, bringing people from different teams together to collaborate.

Governance

There are several ways to set up and run a design system. These tend to define the rules of ownership and change management. Whether the organization is centralized or decentralized, understanding the needs of an organization helps us find the right fit. It also helps us work together to drive positive change. When it comes to steering a design system, following up on the expected outcomes and impact allows us to make the right prioritizations.

"Put the energy to create something more meaningful, more delightful, rather than just getting shit done."

Petri Heiskanen, SVP of Design, Idean

Appendix

A home for useful things

A bit of terminology

Philosophy

A philosophy defines what's right for an organization and the customers it serves.

We believe that each design system is based on a comprehensive understanding of the brand identity, the ecosystem of products and services it provides, the platforms and architecture it relies on, the current culture within the organization, it's a strategy for the future, as well as the pillars of the business.

It's essential that the philosophy is clearly defined before diving into the specifics of a design system. Creating the first series of blueprints requires engaging individuals and units across the organization. Not only will this fast-forward adoption, but it will shine a light on all the different hidden debates. It helps to build a more multi-disciplinary, cross-functional understanding of what truly matters. It will also help identify and prioritize the high-value starting points for a design system.

Principles

Principles bridge the overarching philosophy with the hands-on craft. They are high-level enough to spark iteration and actionable enough to serve as selection criteria.

At first glance, principles often seem to take the form of a highly curated set of keywords or sentences. It becomes clear that principles are also about shared beliefs or particular points of view that truly matter - as well as a range of examples and first-hand experiences on when and how these might best be realized.

Larger organizations may have multiple sets of principles. For example, visual identity and user experience might require their own sets of principles. Principles can be overarching in these larger organizations, and so clarifying the hierarchies and providing contexts of use for each set is essential.

UI foundations

UI foundations make it possible for reusable, ready-made assets to be combined in many ways without the interface and user flow feeling "off" or disconnected.

The first step would be to define the underlying structures, key behaviors, and signature styles. These include:

- Grids
- Colors
- Typographic choices
- The use of motion
- The semantics
- The responsive behaviors
- The connection points to APIs

Ideally, these would also extend to the UX copy, which forms a considerable part of the experience.

These are all the defining practices that come with any particular technology and are most familiar to users.

Reusable assets

Assets are the building blocks and templates that are used to explore and deliver products and services for end users.

Creating, distributing, and evolving UI libraries can form a significant part of a design system initiative, at least when it comes to the aspects of craft. The most powerful examples we've seen blend the boundaries between front-end development and design.

A design system can also be used to influence new ways of working. Distributing templates such as journey maps and service blueprints, plus raising awareness and providing training can help teams focus on the user and further build on business needs.

By definition, reusable assets are going to be used by multiple, if not all teams (or units). It tends to be beneficial for a product team to closely collaborate with design and development operations (if these are in place).

Documentation

Take a bold step and go beyond your initial associations of "documentation."

Think of the types of content you love, the best training you've ever participated in, the clearest and actionable rules. Think of the tools and services that give you just the thing you were looking for, allowing you to move on with your main agenda. Those are the things we should think about when we refer to the documentation.

For design systems, creating a public or semi-public site has become a default form of documentation. It provides an easy-to-distribute, up-to-date, anytime access, onboarding, and learning resource. In this book, we'd like to highlight the other activities that help to produce and curate documentation.

Design

If "design system" wasn't such an established term already, we'd be calling it something else.

Design has become more conceptual than anything. For example, it is no longer perceived merely as a form of giving life to a product, object, or artifact. It has made breakthroughs and now has "a seat at the table" at the highest levels of organizations.

Design (and design thinking in particular) is a mindset, characterized by human-centered empathy and collaborative working. It also means prototyping early and often. All of these are an essential part of creating things that people need and enjoy, whether the result is a service, a product, a process, or a brand.

Products and services

In this book, we tend to use "product" as a shorthand for both products and services.

There also tends to be a in-built bias for digital touchpoints in particular. After all, just getting the mechanisms in place to have the design system takes some time.

It's good to remember that even the smallest tactical UI decisions can raise questions about other aspects, for example, offline steps, business rules, exchanges with service staff, or the available insights on customers, their behavior, and relationship with the brand.

Similarly, the more popular a system becomes, the more legacy there will be. Without a strong vision for the desired offering (both in terms of internal buy-in and customer demand), it will be significantly harder to manage a timeline and other various approaches for rolling out the design system.

Customer and employee experiences

A design system helps create cohesive customer experiences, as well as streamline the design process for employees. If the everyday work experience is "off" within the organization, it lessens the chances for the design system to be successful.

As we learned from our interviews, a design system initiative easily slips into organizational design. There's so much work involved in the internal implementation.

We're all for ensuring that being part of a design system initiative feels worthwhile, even rewarding. However, there's a risk of forgetting about customer insights.

A design system's core team is often highly dependent on other teams, and the stronger the collaboration and shared knowledge are, the more people will see the value for having a design system. system soon starts decreasing in the eyes of the various experts relying on it.

A very short, incomplete, and scattered history of how we've gotten here

Companies start documenting their visual identities in the form of brand manuals, like NASA's graphics design manual created in 1975.

The first, public draft of Web Content Accessibility Guidelines (WCAG) is published in 1998.

Gary Hamel's "The Future of Management," is published in 2007. The must-win challenge for continued innovation is framed, among other things, as a need to "create a democracy for ideas" through communities free of past bureaucracies.

Managing and distributing code-heavy projects becomes easier. Github is founded in 2007, starting its march over the years to become one of the go-to-platforms for developers.

It's all about agile, lean, and co. The autonomy of teams increases significantly, at least in some ways. Organizational dependencies are never that far away.

Donella H. Meadows' "Thinking in Systems," is published posthumously in 2008, serving as a primer to systems thinking and encouraging us to apply it to tackle the real-life problems that tend to seem most daunting.

Brad Frost's blog, "Atomic Design," turns into a book in 2013. Brad Frost makes the term "design system" more widely known for digital creatives.

IBM Design Language is launched in 2014. In addition to the shared guidelines, a significant change initiative takes place within the organization, evening out the previously low design-to-developer ratio. Google's Material Design, first launched in 2014, sets a specific benchmark for design systems, and many intended users. It provides a tremendous leap forward for the Android operating system.

Smashing Design book on Design systems by Alla Kholmatova is published in late 2017, reflecting an ongoing appetite for practical manuals on how to get started with a design system initiative.

Thought leaders and interview participants

Friends and extended network

David Kendall
Principal, UX Design, AT&T

Emanuela Damiani
Senior UX Product Designer, Mozilla

Hayley Hughes
Design Lead, Airbnb

Jason Cyr
Director, Design Transformation, Cisco

Jeoff Wilks
Director, Carbon Design System, IBM

J F Grossen
VP of Design, Global, HERE Technologies

Paul Roberts
Global Digital Director, Centrica

Joseph McLaughlin
Partner, Director of Design, Microsoft

Josh Baron
Senior Principal Product Designer, Dell

Marie Petit
Leader of the UX Chapter, Crédit Agricole Technologies & Services

Marjukka Mäkelä
Head of UX Design, Digital ABB

Matthew Gottschalk
Design Operations Manager, Centrica

Nick Cochran
Design Practices Lead, ExxonMobil

Nathan Mitchell
Design Manager and Chief Interaction Designer, National Instruments

Appendix

Idean experts

Audrey Hacq
Design Lead,
Idean France

Christian Aminoff
Creative Director,
Idean Helsinki

Corne van Dooren
Art Director, Idean
Netherlands

Elisa Pyrhönen
Senior Service
Designer, Idean
Helsinki

Jess Leitch
Design Principal,
Idean Palo Alto

Jordan Fisher
Design Director,
Idean UK

Jules Mahé
Lead UI Designer,
Idean France

Karolina Boremalm
Managing UX
Designer, Idean
Sweden

Matias Vaara
Creative Director, Idean Helsinki

Kevin van der Bijl
Design Lead, Idean Netherlands

Sampo Jalasto
Head of Design, Idean Palo Alto

Petri Heiskanen
SVP of Design, Idean Helsinki

Robin Klein Schiphorst
Design Lead, Idean Norway

Appendix **214**

Adobe

Cisco Guzman
Director, Product Management, Adobe XD, Adobe

Shawn Ceris
Director of Design, Adobe Design, Adobe

Idean studios

Looking to get started with design systems? We have studios around the globe, with experience solving problems in just about every industry. Get in touch and let's discuss what we can achieve together.

hi@idean.com

Europe

Barcelona, Spain
Avinguda Diagonal, 199
08018 Barcelona
barcelona@idean.com

Bergen, Norway
Nordre Nøstekaien 1
5011 Bergen
bergen@idean.com

Berlin, Germany
Oberwallstrasse 6
10117 Berlin
berlin@idean.com

Gothenburg, Sweden
Grafiska vägen 2,
412 63 Gothenburg
gothenburg@idean.com

Helsinki, Finland
Kauppaneuvoksentie 8,
00200 Helsinki
helsinki@idean.com

London, UK
Victoria House
1 Leonard Circus, EC2A 4DQ
london@idean.com

Madrid, Spain
Calle Puerto de Somport, 9
28050 Madrid
madrid@idean.com

Malmö, Sweden
Nordenskiöldsgatan 8
211 19 Malmö
malmo@idean.com

Montpellier, France
L'Orée des mas,
Avenue du golf,
34670 Baillargues
contact.france@idean.com

Oslo, Norway
Karenslyst Allé 16 D,
0278 Oslo
oslo@idean.com

Paris, France
8 rue Cambacérès,
75008 Paris
contact.france@idean.com

Stavanger, Norway
Maskinveien 24,
4033 Stavanger
stavanger@idean.com

Stockholm, Sweden
Fleminggatan 18,
112 26 Stockholm
stockholm@idean.com

Tampere, Finland
Kuninkaankatu 22,
33210 Tampere
tampere@idean.com

Utrecht, Netherlands
Reykjavikplein 1,
3543 Utrecht
contact.netherlands@idean.com

Valencia, Spain
Av. del Marqués de Sotelo, 6
46002 Valencia
valencia@idean.com

Appendix

USA

Austin
713 E 6th St,
TX 78701
austin@idean.com

Palo Alto
214 Homer Ave,
CA 94301
paloalto@idean.com

San Francisco
427 Brannan St,
CA 94107
sanfrancisco@idean.com

Asia

Shanghai
28F, SML Center, No.610,
Xujiahui Road,
200025

Singapore
6 Battery Road #14-05/06,
049909

Contributors

We'd also like to thank those who helped us run the interviews, synthesise the findings, add their comments, draft content and visualizations, run edits, or otherwise contribute to the making of this book.

Audrey Hacq
Ben Lambert
Benedikte Torgersen
Carel Coenraad
Charlotta Turku
Christian Aminoff
Elisa Pyrhönen
Emmi Makkonen
Felipe Villarreal
Franco Papeschi
Jamie Weston
Jordan Winick
Josselin Despinay
Jules Mahé
Jin Kim
Karolina Boremalm
Laura Immonen-Beatty
Maria Knutsson
Maria Niiniharju
Markus Ruottu
Matias Ljubica
Mindy Reyes
Pekka Puhakka
Petri Heiskanen
Pierre-Henri Clouin
Robin Pettersson
Sampo Jalasto
Victor Janhagen
+ others

Appendix **220**

Your notes

Plan, write, sketch, and scribble.

Appendix

Appendix

Hack the Design System is about the human aspects of design systems, but it also talks about the challenges around buy-in, people and resources, communication, and maintenance.

Our insights show that product teams using design systems are launching digital products and services 50% faster than those organizations that don't have a design system in place.

This book is filled with tangible perspectives and recommendations around building design systems, with industry case stories and real-world challenges.

idean.com/learn

Printed in Poland
by Amazon Fulfillment
Poland Sp. z o.o., Wrocław